THE GREAT COMMISSION

DOABLE

THOUGHTS ON REACHING OUR WORLD IN OUR GENERATION

Delron Shirley

2013

Cover design by Jeremy Shirley

Table of Contents

For permission to quote material from this book, contact:

Delron Shirley
3210 Cathedral Spires Dr.
Colorado Springs, CO 80904
teachallnations@msn.com
www.teachallnationsmission.com

Challenging Giants

For some reason that I don't remember at the moment, we decided to skip taking the ring road that circles around the city of Kathmandu; instead, we drove through the heart of the residential area to get to the other side of the city. As we twisted and turned on one lane after another on what seemed like an endless pilgrimage through the labyrinth of shacks and dwellings, my mind was racing far faster than our Jeep. As I canvassed the myriad of houses and the teeming mass of people, I wondered how in the world we could ever reach them all with the gospel. After almost two decades of ministry in Nepal, I had seen the churches grow from just a few underground meeting places to a number of large well-established congregations. The Christian population had mushroomed from a handful of believers to a phenomenon that was frequently reported in Christian magazines as the fastest growing segment in the Body of Christ. In fact, until that day, I was somewhat proud of what was happening in Nepal and the fact that I was privileged to be part of it. But, this little side trip brought my whole view of the ministry in Nepal into a new focus: no matter how much had been accomplished, it still seemed like the proverbial drop in the bucket compared to what remained to be done. That same gnawing feeling escalated to a new level on the flight home. As founder and president of Teach All Nations Mission, I somehow wanted to pat myself on the back for having ministered in over three dozen countries and on every continent except Antarctica. Yet, as I endured the day-and-a-half journey from Asia back to the US, I couldn't keep from experiencing a certain unsettled feeling about the number of nations and the millions of people that I was flying above without having any opportunity of sharing the gospel with them. Certainly, I could celebrate the victories I had witnessed in the two cities I had just visited in Nepal, but that celebration was somehow dampened by the fact that so many other cities and villages in Nepal had not been touched and that we had not been able to reach all those souls we had driven

1

past within the cities where we had been ministering. Burdened by the sensation that I was simply flying over whole nations, unable to touch them, I couldn't help but wonder if it was really possible that we could ever fulfill Jesus' directive to take His message to everyone in the whole world.

I was facing a giant of a challenge, one as big as the whole world and as extensive as the Earth's total population. As you read these lines today, somewhere on this vast globe, an unsuspecting mother has just given birth to the planet's seven billionth occupant. And, barring some global holocaust, it won't be long until that number is eight billion, then nine billion, and even more. After all, in grade school, I learned that the human population was three and a half billion – only half of what it is today. It is almost unimaginable that it took all the way until the beginning of the nineteenth century for the human population to cross the one billion threshold; yet, it is expected to have reached the ten billion mark before the end of this present century. In order to get our heads around exactly how many people seven billion really is, let's imagine that we are going to have roll call of the entire population of the world and we give each person just one second to introduce himself. That simple task would take two hundred twenty-two years! Starting right now, we wouldn't finish until the year 2233!

How was I to take on such a monster? The answer, I knew, would be found in only one place – the scriptures. So, I turned to the familiar story of giant fighting in I Samuel chapter seventeen – the story of David and Goliath. Knowing that there is usually more than meets the eye in a Bible story, I determined to study the details and read between the lines in an attempt to look beneath the surface for clues to what made David able to attack and take down his nemesis.

The first detail that I noticed hidden in plain sight was the difference between the ways everyone else and David assessed themselves. In at least nine places, I found the Israelites and Philistines alike referring to *the men of Israel, the servants of Saul, the army of Israel*, and simply *Israel*. (verses

2

2, 3, 8, 10, 11, 19, 21, 24, 25) Yet, when David looked at the situation, he saw it from a totally different perspective; he saw himself as part of *the army of the living God.* (verses 26, 36) While everyone else had only a natural vantage point from which to evaluate the situation, David was able to see it from a divine perspective. From a human's point of view, the giant was huge; but, from a heavenly perspective, the giant was no big deal. In this same context, I was able to see a totally different perspective in the way David looked at the king's reward for fighting the giant. When the young shepherd boy appeared on the scene at the Valley of Elah, he was told by three different sources that the king had issued a monetary reward, the privilege of marrying his daughter, and tax exemption to anyone who would fight and kill Goliath. (verses 25, 27, 30) But, the interesting thing about this offer is that it was not enough to stimulate even one soldier to take up his weapon against the giant. David, on the other hand, had a totally different motivation for "stepping up to the plate" that day. In verse twenty-nine, after having heard the king's offer twice, David asked the question, *Is there not a cause?* For him, neither the money, the bride, nor the tax exemption was a significant cause. In fact, the following chapter suggests that David did not claim his prize money in that he sent a message to King Saul indicating that he was too poor to pay the marriage dowry. (verse 23) The very fact that a dowry was required suggests that the king was actually reneging on his offer of tax exemption. In addition, David's question, *Who am I...that I should be the son-in-law of the king?* (verse 18) proves that the marriage promise had been forfeited. Otherwise, David would have readily acknowledged that he was due the honor as a result of having confronted the giant. Instead, for David, the stimulus for taking up Goliath's challenge was that an uncircumcised Philistine had defied the armies of the living God. (verses 26, 36) Here again, David was different from the others in that his motivation and purpose was not on the human level of money, marriage, or taxes; it was on the divine level of defending the name and reputation of the living God. The first key to David's success was that he had a God-sized purpose.

As I continued to read through the details of the story, I noticed another truth totally concealed in open view – David had a scripturally inspired plan of attack. When he confronted his adversary, he announced that his intention was to cut off the giant's head and to feed his flesh to the birds of the air. (verse 46) Although the story does not specifically tell us how he developed this plan, I feel confident that it must have been inspired by the promise in Deuteronomy 28:7 that, when our enemies come against us one way, they will have to flee seven directions. Certainly, David was impressed that, although there were thousands of Philistines on the field that day, only one was challenging him. While there was the possibility of attacks from a thousand different directions at once, his opponent was coming at him from only one angle. Surely, such a scenario must have quickened the biblical promise in his heart. Next, the young shepherd must have questioned how the singular opponent could flee away in seven different directions. Then the answer flashed into his mind, "If I cut off his head and let his body fall to the ground, that will be two directions. And if the birds of the air that consume his flesh fly away to the north, south, east, west, and straight up into the air, that will be five more directions. The total will be seven different prophetic directions!" David's second key was a scripturally inspired plan.

Yet, there was one more factor to be discovered in the giant-conquering story, and it was again hidden in plain view in the story. This detail had to do with what David held in his hand as he challenged the giant. Since I made this discovery, I've asked audiences all across Asia, Africa, and America to tell me what the shepherd boy had in his hand when he went after Goliath, and no one has ever given me the correct answer. Everyone mentions the sling, and most mention the five smooth stones, but no one has ever told me that he also held a stick. Interestingly enough, it is the stick in his hand, not the sling or the stones, that is actually intended to be the focus of attention in this part of the story. (verse 40) In seeking the significance of the stick in David's hand, we must go back to

4

the story of another shepherd who was sent out to fight another giant and do exploits for the Lord. As Moses wandered through the desert, caring for his father-in-law's sheep, he encountered a burning bush from which he heard the voice of God Himself sending him off to single-handedly face the emperor of the mightiest nation on the planet – an even more formidable foe than the one who stood before David in the Valley of Elah. When Moses replied that he simply couldn't take on such a gargantuan task, the Lord asked him one unpretentious question, "What is in your hand?" (Exodus 4:2) When Moses answered that it was a stick, God directed that he throw it on the ground, and it turned into a snake. After God revealed to Moses that there was literally supernatural power in his hand, Moses actually changed the name of his stick to *the rod of God*. (Exodus 4:20, 17:9) It was with this stick in his hand that Moses made his appearance before Pharaoh and began to challenge the most powerful government and army on the planet. It was with this rod in his hand – and occasionally in the hand of his spokesman Aaron – that Moses brought plagues and devastation upon the resistant nation and eventually opened up the Red Sea as a way of escape for the Israelites. (Exodus 7:19, 8:5-6, 8:16-17, 9:22-23, 10:12-13, 14:16) Undoubtedly, the young shepherd took a lesson from the life of the older shepherd as he determined to take his staff with him when he went into battle with the giant. Notice that the story in I Samuel actually focuses on the stick in David's hand in that it was only the stick, not the sling or stones, that Goliath noticed as the shepherd boy approached. (verse 43) Having mentioned the stick, Goliath then proceeded to curse David in the name of his pagan gods. David's response was that even though the Philistine came against him with a sword, a spear, and a javelin, he was coming against the giant with the name of the Lord of hosts, the God of the armies of Israel. Then, for good measure, he added that it was the God that Goliath had defied. In looking at the parallels set up in the conversation between the antagonist and the protagonist, it seems obvious that David perceived the stick in his hand to be symbolic of the power of God just as Moses had realized that his staff demonstrated the authority of God in his conflict with his foe. The stick in David's hand was his connection to the supernatural power of God needed to guide his sling and hurl his projectile to its target. David's third key to victory was the supernatural power of God upon his life.

Taking on the Great Commission

A God-sized purpose, a scripturally inspired plan, and a supernatural power – these three keys enabled David to take on Goliath; and I knew that I would need these same three keys in order to conquer the giant that loomed before me. Having found what I considered to be the secret to conquering giants, I next turned to the Great Commission, the giant that had set me on this quest in the first place, with the intent of seeing if Jesus might have hidden these same three clues within His directive. The first step in searching out these keys was to identify the multiple presentations of the Great Commission.

Five different times, Jesus commissioned His disciples into their ministries. Many people assume that He gave the Great Commission only once and it was recorded with different emphases by the gospel writers; however, by carefully studying the post-resurrection appearances of the Savior, we can see that they occurred at different places and at different times during the time between Jesus' resurrection and His ascension. In reality, He was constantly challenging His followers with this mission.

Matthew 28:16-20 records the appearance of Jesus to the disciples on a mountain in Galilee.

Then the eleven disciples went away into Galilee, into a mountain where Jesus had appointed them. And when they saw him, they worshipped him: but some doubted. And Jesus came and spake unto them, saying, All power is given unto me in heaven and in earth. Go ye therefore, and teach all nations, baptizing them in the name of the Father, and of the Son, and of the Holy Ghost: Teaching them to observe all things whatsoever I have commanded you: and, lo, I am with you alway, even unto the end of the world. Amen.

Mark 16:14-18 describes an appearance while they were having a meal, apparently in Jerusalem.

Afterward he appeared unto the eleven as they sat at meat, and upbraided them with their unbelief and hardness of heart, because they believed not them which had seen him after he was risen. And he said unto them, Go ye into all the world, and preach the gospel to every creature. He that believeth and is baptized shall be saved; but he that believeth not shall be damned. And these signs shall follow them that believe; In my name shall they cast out devils; they shall speak with new tongues; They shall take up serpents; and if they drink any deadly thing, it shall not hurt them; they shall lay hands on the sick, and they shall recover.

Luke 24:36-49 recounts the first manifestation of Jesus to His disciples as a group after the resurrection.

And as they thus spake, Jesus himself stood in the midst of them, and saith unto them, Peace be unto you. But they were terrified and affrighted, and supposed that they had seen a spirit. And he said unto them, Why are ye troubled? and why do thoughts arise in your hearts? Behold my hands and my feet, that it is I myself: Handle me, and see; for a spirit hath not flesh and bones, as ye see me have. And when he had thus spoken, he shewed them his hands and his feet. And while they yet believed not for joy, and wondered, he said unto them, Have ye here any meat? And they gave him a piece of a broiled fish, and of an honeycomb. And he took it, and did eat before them. And he said unto them, These are the words which I spake unto you, while I was yet with you, that all things must be fulfilled, which are written in the law of Moses, and in the prophets, and in the psalms concerning me. Then opened he their understanding, that they might understand the scriptures, And said unto them, Thus is it written, and thus it behooved Christ to suffer, and to rise from the dead the third day: And that repentance and remission of sins should be preached in his name among all nations, beginning at Jerusalem. And ye are witnesses of these things. And, behold, I send the promise of my Father upon you: but tarry ye in the city of Jerusalem, until ye be endued with power from on high.

John 20:21-22 records Jesus' visit with the disciples on the evening of the first Easter.

Then said Jesus to them again, Peace be unto you: as my Father hath sent me, even so send I you. And when he had said this, he breathed on them, and saith unto them, Receive ye the Holy Ghost.

Acts 1:3-9 documents His final conversation with the disciples on the Mount of Olives at the time of the ascension.

To whom also he shewed himself alive after his passion by many infallible proofs, being seen of them forty days, and speaking of the things pertaining to the kingdom of God: And being assembled together with them, commanded them that they should not depart from Jerusalem, but wait for the promise of the Father, which, saith he, ye have heard of me. For John truly baptized with water; but ye shall be baptized with the Holy Ghost not many days hence. When they therefore were come together, they asked of him, saying, Lord, wilt thou at this time restore again the kingdom to Israel? And he said unto them, It is not for you to know the times of the seasons, which the Father hath put in his own power. But ye shall receive power, after that the Holy Ghost is come upon you: and ye shall be witnesses unto me both in Jerusalem, and in all Judea, and in Samaria, and unto the uttermost part of the earth. And when he had spoken these things, while they beheld, he was taken up; and a cloud received him out of their sight.

It didn't take much searching through these five different passages to find the God-sized purpose. In fact, it was the enormity of the challenge of reaching each and every person with the gospel that had originally sent me on the present quest. But as I analyzed these passages more carefully, I discovered that there was a three-fold definition of this God-sized purpose wrapped inside these passages – the same purpose as expressed by the Apostle Paul when he spelled out the function of the ministry in Ephesians 4:12. Although many Bible teachers interpret this passage in different ways, it seems evident from the Greek structure that Paul intended there to be a three-fold delineation of the Christian purpose: for the perfecting of the saints, for the work of the ministry, and for the edifying of the Body of Christ, each segment of which directly correlates with Jesus' directives in the Great Commission. The ministry of maturing the saints is accomplished through discipleship as expressed in Matthew. The work of the ministry is accomplished through the manifestation of the signs and wonders as listed in Mark's version of the Great Commission. The edifying – or building up and increasing – of the Body of Christ is accomplished through the evangelism implicit in every pronouncement of the Commission.

The scripturally inspired plan of the Great Commission also came in three distinct parts: witnessing (mentioned in Luke and Acts), evangelism (central to Mark's account), and disciple-making (the focus of Matthew's version). While witnessing is a simple testimony of what we have seen and experienced, evangelism is a presentation of the gospel message with the intent of bringing the hearer to a point of making the decision to place his faith in Christ, and disciple-making is the process of helping nurture the new converts into fully mature believers. Witnessing is not at all difficult and doesn't require any specialized training. Let's take an example on the natural level to help understand this point. If you were to witness an automobile accident and were to be called into court to testify about the incident, you could not claim that you should be excused from appearing due to the fact that you are not an automobile mechanic. The judge would insist that you don't have to understand all about how an automobile works in order to testify about the collision of the two vehicles. The judge might then demand that your testimony is necessary because someone was injured in the accident. At that point, if you were to try to insist that you could not possibly testify since you are not a medical doctor, he would again disregard your request on the grounds that you don't need to understand all about the human body to tell the court that you saw a person bleeding from cuts he received in the accident. In the same way, we do not need to be theologians to witness about what has happened in our lives. Likewise, evangelism is not really specialized either. In fact, the Bible makes the point that the early Christians were not highly educated (Acts 4:13, I Corinthians 1:26); yet, they turned their world upside down with their gospel message (Acts 17:6). All evangelism requires is a heartfelt experience with God that gives you enough passion to <u>want</u> <u>to</u> <u>share</u> your faith with others and a simple enough understanding of the salvation experience so that you <u>can</u> <u>share</u> it with them. (Acts 4:13) As I considered how easy the first two elements of Jesus' three-fold plan are, I realized that we have traditionally made a distinction at this point by assuming that discipleship requires specific training and special knowledge of the scriptures, limiting the number of qualified people who can fulfill this part of the plan. Yet, I instinctively felt that this assumption might just be "the fly in the ointment" that has hindered us from really being able to fully accomplish the Great Commission. After all, the commandment to disciple the nations was left to the same unlearned and ignorant men as were the other two parts of the plan. (Acts 4:13)

The third aspect of David's success in facing the giant was that he had a supernatural power. I discovered that there is a promise of supernatural empowerment repeated throughout the statements of the Great Commission. In fact, there is more than just a promise of power; there is a promise of actual divine assistance and enablement. In Matthew's account, Jesus promised, *Lo, I am with you alway, even unto the end of the world.* (verse 28:20) In Luke's account, He told them to wait for the fulfillment of the promise of the Father. (verse 24:49) In the Acts account, He told the disciples that they would be empowered by the Holy Spirit (verse 1:8), a promise that is apparently intended in Mark's account even though the exact term is not used (verses 16:17-18). John's record of the Great Commission lists the involvement of the total Trinity: the Father sent Jesus, Jesus is sending the disciples, and the disciples are to receive the Holy Spirit. When all these passages are considered at one time, we see a remarkable truth emerging – the total Trinity is involved in empowering us to ensure our success as we go forth to undertake the task Jesus left with us!

Divine Teamwork

In order to see how all three persons of the Godhead are personally involved in helping us complete the task Jesus has given us, let's take a look at I Corinthians chapter twelve. Even though your Bible may list this chapter as a discussion of spiritual gifts, it is actually much more. You may notice that the word "gifts" in verse one is in italics. This means that the word is not actually in the original Greek text. It was added by the translator for what he thought would bring clarity. Actually, this addition confused the meaning of the chapter rather than clarifying it. If we were to translate the verse literally, it would read simply, "I would not have you ignorant concerning spirituals." However, a bit smoother reading might be, "I would not have you ignorant concerning spiritual things." Paul does discuss the gifts of the Spirit in this chapter; however, that is not the limit of his interest. He also explains spiritual administrations and spiritual operations.

> *There are diversities of gifts, but the same Spirit. And there are differences of administrations, but the same Lord. And there are diversities of operations, but it is the same God which worketh all in all. But the manifestation of the Spirit is given to every man to profit withal.* (verses 4-7)

Notice that Paul begins by mentioning that the Holy Spirit will give us gifts – supernatural abilities to do things that we as humans would never otherwise be capable of doing. He even gives us a listing of these gifts in verses eight through ten. Next, Paul tells us that the Lord Jesus gives us various administrations. From Ephesians 4:11, we can understand that Jesus is in charge of placing individual believers into positions so that they can minister with the supernatural gifts that the Holy Spirit has placed inside of them. Paul goes on to give us a list of some of these ministry positions (or administrations) in verses twenty-eight through thirty. Finally, the Apostle turns to the role of the Father and says that He gives us a diversity of operations. Here, Paul is telling us that it is the Father who puts godly motivations in our lives, enabling us to function in the positions in which Jesus has placed us, using the giftings that the Holy Spirit has placed in our lives. As you would expect, Paul goes on to give us a list of these operations just as he has given us a list of the gifts and of the administrations, *And now abideth faith, hope, charity, these three; but the greatest of these is charity.* (verse 13:13) Notice how often chapter thirteen emphasizes the futility of the gifts and administrations without the operation of these godly characteristics (verses 1-3); whereas, verse 12:7 guarantees that there will be universal benefit when all three elements supplied by all three members of the Trinity are in alignment.

Notice how Jesus had preannounced all this in the last discourse He had with His disciples after the Last Supper. He promised them that they would do supernatural things – even things that exceeded His own miracles. He told them that the key would be the indwelling of the full Trinity in their lives and that love would be the determining factor to having this presence of God in their lives. He also emphasized that there was a divine realization that would be hidden from some but readily accessible to others. In addition, He associated this whole process with the ability to receive His peace, a peace that the world cannot give. All these points will become very meaningful a little later when we begin to unwrap some of the truths concerning the role of sons and daughters of peace in spreading the gospel.

Verily, verily, I say unto you, He that believeth on me, the works that I do shall he do also; and greater works than these shall he do; because I go unto my Father. And whatsoever ye shall ask in my name, that will I do, that the Father may be glorified in the Son. If ye shall ask any thing in my name, I will do it. If ye love me, keep my commandments. And I will pray the Father, and he shall give you another Comforter, that he may abide with you for ever; Even the Spirit of truth; whom the world cannot receive, because it seeth him not, neither knoweth him: but ye know him; for he dwelleth with you, and shall be in you. I will not leave you comfortless: I will come to you. Yet a little while, and the world seeth me no more; but ye see me: because I live, ye shall live also. At that day ye shall know that I am in my Father, and ye in me, and I in you. He that hath my commandments, and keepeth them, he it is that loveth me: and he that loveth me shall be loved of my Father, and I will love him, and will manifest myself to him. Judas saith unto him, not Iscariot, Lord, how is it that thou wilt manifest thyself unto us, and not unto the world? Jesus answered and said unto him, If a man love me, he will keep my words: and my Father will love him, and we will come unto him, and make our abode with him. He that loveth me not keepeth not my sayings: and the word which ye hear is not mine, but the Father's which sent me. These things have I spoken unto you, being yet present with you. But the Comforter, which is the Holy Ghost, whom the Father will send in my name, he shall teach you all things, and bring all things to your remembrance, whatsoever I have said unto you. Peace I leave with you, my peace I give unto you: not as the world giveth, give I unto you. Let not your heart be troubled, neither let it be afraid. (John 14:12-27)

This promise of divine help was actualized in the lives of the first disciples. In addition to the numerous examples we could cite from the accounts recorded in Acts, at least two scriptures specifically say that God actively did His part:

And they went forth, and preached every where, the Lord working with them, and confirming the word with signs following. Amen. (Mark 16:20)
God also bearing them witness, both with signs and wonders, and with divers miracles, and gifts of the

15

Holy Ghost, according to his own will. (Hebrews 2:4)

In fact, the reality of divine involvement is so preeminent that some authors have made the clever play on words, based on the fact that the prefix *co* means "with," that Jesus left us with a co̲mmission – not just a mission – because He was determined to be part of the team. As a matter of fact, this is exactly what Jesus was intending when He invited us to be yoked together with Him in His yoke. (Matthew 11:29-30) What an unbeatable team!

In truth, we do better to say that we are on God's team rather than suggesting that He is on our team. Paul clarified the order of significance of team members in I Corinthians 3:9 when he wrote, *For we are labourers together with God: ye are God's husbandry, ye are God's building.* In Philippians 2:13, he made it crystal clear that any motivation and any ability to function was not from our side, but totally from God's provision, *For it is God which worketh in you both to will and to do of his good pleasure.* In Romans 15:18, he spoke of what Christ had accomplished through him, and it was in Galatians 2:20 that he spelled out the same truth with unequivocal clarity when he penned the words, I am crucified with Christ: nevertheless I live; yet not I, but Christ liveth in me: and the life which I now live in the flesh I live by the faith of the Son of God, who loved me, and gave himself for me.

In fact, God is much more interested in the Great Commission than any of us as His team members are. He often takes the initiative to "get the ball in play" and then turns to His team members to bring in the score. The story of Cornelius in Acts chapter ten and the story of Saul of Tarsus in Acts chapter nine are great examples of this truth. Notice how Cornelius had a divine encounter and was given a message to go to Simon the tanner's house to look for a man named Simon Peter – even before Peter was made aware that he was a player in this particular game. The same thing happened to Ananias when God had pre-committed him to go on what seemed like a suicide mission to find Saul of Tarsus even before he was

16

asked to join the match. Current history is also filled with similar stories.

The first personal experience of this nature happened when I was a college student back in the 1970s, during the hippie revolution when "sex, drugs, and rock and roll" was the mantra for the day. One day I picked up a young girl who was hitchhiking near the campus. She only needed a lift for a few blocks, but that short ride put her on the most exciting journey of her life – the road to heaven. When she got into my car, she made a comment about the "God loves you" decal on my dashboard. As I began to tell her about the plan of salvation, she shared her story. As an atheist, she had rejected everything anyone had ever shared with her about God or the need for her soul to be saved. However, while experimenting with LSD, she had remained "high" while all the others who were "tripping" with her had come "down." In her drug-induced state, the only explanation she could imagine was that she was dead while all the others were still alive. When she did eventually come "down," she said that something inside of her cried out, "Thank God, I'm alive." At that moment, she knew that she must have a soul and that there must be a God. That divine encounter had prepared her for the conversation I was to share with her that day.

The first time I encountered one of these divine "handoffs" in which a person who was totally unfamiliar with the Christian faith had a preparatory visitation occurred in India. When I walked into a Christian bookstore, the clerk pointed my attention to a picture of Jesus that hung in the front window and said that he wanted to tell me about what had just happened. A Hindu man had come into the store a few days before, asking if he could meet the man in the picture. When the shopkeeper explained that it was a painting of a man who lived many years ago, the customer was perplexed, saying that he had seen the man in his dreams several nights in a row and that he knew he needed to meet him. When he saw the painting, he understood that his quest for this mystery man had finally been fruitful. The store clerk, of course, led this hungry soul to salvation.

The most dramatic story I have encountered came from the remote mountains of Nepal where one of my friends was doing door-to-door evangelism. One man he met in a very isolated mountain village had been having visions of the various Hindu gods. In fact, he had filled numerous volumes with handwritten narratives of all the stories and revelations he had received about these deities. Then, one night, he had a vision in which he was directed that he would be given a revelation about a more powerful deity if he would destroy all the journals he had written about the lesser deities. When he burned the other logbooks, he began to have visions and dreams about a God that he had never learned about before. He wrote the stories and revelations about this new god, but didn't have a name for him – until my friend came to his hut and introduced him to Jesus and showed him that the same stories he was recording had already been written down almost two thousand years before!

A little old lady from our church in Indiana traveled into the hinterlands of the Philippines to share the gospel in the unreached villages. In one of these villages, she met a very elderly man who had lived far beyond the normal life expectancy of the people in his area. When Aunty Ruth shared the message of Jesus with the old man, he readily responded with the words, "So that's His name!" He explained that he already knew about this true God through dreams and visions, but had never had an opportunity to know who He was. Only a few days after Aunty introduced him to Jesus, the old man passed away.

Andrew Wommack, the president of the Bible college where I teach, tells the story of introducing himself to a receptionist at a business he was visiting. When she asked what business he was in, Andrew responded that he was a minister. Her next question was, "For whom?" When Andrew replied that he was a minister for Jesus Christ, she immediately interrupted, "Well, then you're the man!" Of course, he

18

questioned her, "What man?" She answered by telling her story. As a Buddhist, she had been going through her religious rituals the night before but felt as if what she was doing was in vain. So she simply prayed, "God, I know that You are real, but I'm not sure who You are. Please show Yourself to me." Instantly, a ball of light invaded her room and a voice spoke to her, "Tomorrow, I'll send a man to tell you who I am." God personally took the divine initiative to reach this woman, but He left the job of scoring the point to one of His ministers. God was <u>working</u> <u>with</u> Andrew Wommack just as He did with the early disciples. (Mark 16:20)

Today, there are incredible stories like the ones I've just shared, mostly coming from nations behind the Koran Curtain where Muslim men and women are having supernatural dreams and visions that initiate their quest for the One True God. Because I had heard so many stories about these divine visitations, I decided to investigate a little and asked the audience when I was ministering in the country of Niger, which is almost one hundred percent Islamic, if any of them had had such supernatural dreams and visions. To my surprise almost one fourth of the congregation raised their hands!

God truly is taking the initiative. (John 14:6) He is even more adamant about the Great Commission than we are (II Peter 3:9), but He always passes the ball to His human team members to score the point. Knowing that God is the primary player on the team does take some of the pressure off of us because we realize that we don't have to do it on our own. At the same time, we still need to be vigilant to make our move when the ball is served into our court.

It is teamwork that makes the dream work. Notice that every time that the Great Commission was given, Jesus was speaking to the whole group of His disciples. Additionally, it seems almost symbolic that we have to hear from each of the evangelists in order to understand this point; they are working together as a team to give us this truth. First Corinthians chapter twelve makes it unequivocally clear that these promises from God are not for individuals alone, but for the Body of Christ as a whole. If we want to fulfill the Great Commission, we must learn to work together as the church universal – because no one person has everything it takes to get the job done. Yet, all the members of the entire Body of Christ working together will have everything – and even more than enough (Ephesians 3:20, II Corinthians 9:8) – to accomplish the Lord's directive.

But all these worketh that one and the selfsame Spirit, dividing to every man severally as he will. For as the body is one, and hath many members, and all the members of that one body, being many, are one body: so also is Christ. For by one Spirit are we all baptized into one body, whether we be Jews or Gentiles, whether we be bond or free; and have been all made to drink into one Spirit. For the body is not one member, but many. If the foot shall say, Because I am not the hand, I am not of the body; is it therefore not of the body? And if the ear shall say, Because I am not the eye, I am not of the body; is it therefore not of the body? If the whole body were an eye, where were the hearing? If the whole were hearing, where were the smelling? But now hath God set the members every one of them in the body, as it hath pleased him. And if they were all one member, where were the body? But now are they many members, yet but one body. And the eye cannot say unto the hand, I have no need of thee: nor again the head to the feet, I have no need of you. Nay, much more those members of the body, which seem to be more feeble, are necessary: And those members of the body, which we think to be less honourable, upon these we bestow more abundant honour; and our uncomely parts have more abundant comeliness. For our comely parts have no need: but God hath tempered the body together, having given more abundant honour to that part which lacked: That there should be no schism in the body; but that the members should have the same care one for another. And whether one member suffer, all the members suffer with it; or one member be honoured, all the members rejoice with it. Now ye are the body of Christ, and members in particular. (I Corinthians 12:11-27)

The same call to cooperation among the team members in order to complete the task rings out from scripture after scripture (Romans 12:4-5; Ephesians 2:16, 4:4; Philippians 1:27; Colossians 3:15), and Paul makes a special effort to acknowledge that he is a team player, dependent upon his teammates (Romans 16:3, 16:9; Philippians 4:3; Philemon 1:24). There was never any suggestion that the task was to be undertaken as an individual project by one minister, church, mission organization, ministry, or para-church organization. The Great Commission is the challenge of the Body of Christ as a whole. One thing that we have to realize is that the presence of leadership is key to the difference between a mob and an army, a crowd and a team, a multitude and disciples, and sheep without a shepherd and a flock. Historically, the problem that has kept the church from being able to fully function as the Body that Jesus intended it to be is that leaders become self-absorbed and self-limiting, building their own empires rather than the kingdom of God. If we can get beyond that point and begin to live and work as a team, there will be no limit to what we can accomplish – even fulfilling the Great Commission. If we all pray for one another, support one another, and share each other's vision, we will discover that the Great Commission actually is doable.

As we look at the condition of the church today, we may ask if it is really possible that we could ever experience such unity and teamwork. I would suggest that we had better leave the answer to God like the prophet at the valley of dry bones did in Ezekiel chapter thirty-seven. God's answer to him was that he should prophesy to the bones even though they were scattered and lifeless. As the prophet continued to speak, the bones began to come together and take on flesh. Eventually, they became individual soldiers and even stood up, full of the breath of life. But, notice what happened next: they were no longer disjointed bones, they were not even individual soldiers, and they became an army – one functioning unit made up of many members under solid leadership, operating in true teamwork – the key to making the Great Commission doable!

Sent

When John the Beloved recorded the Great Commission, he remembered the words of Jesus stating that He was sending the church into the world in the same way that the Father sent Him.

Then the same day at evening, being the first day of the week, when the doors were shut where the disciples were assembled for fear of the Jews, came Jesus and stood in the midst, and saith unto them, Peace be unto you. And when he had so said, he shewed unto them his hands and his side. Then were the disciples glad, when they saw the Lord. Then said Jesus to them again, Peace be unto you: as my Father hath sent me, even so send I you. And when he had said this, he breathed on them, and saith unto them, Receive ye the Holy Ghost: Whose soever sins ye remit, they are remitted unto them; and whose soever sins ye retain, they are retained. (John 20:19-23)

There may be many ways to interpret exactly what He meant by this statement, but I would like to suggest that we can find some powerful meaning for the wording by looking at Paul's writings in Galatians 4:4-5:

But when the fulness of the time was come, God sent forth his Son, made of a woman, made under the law, To redeem them that were under the law, that we might receive the adoption of sons.

Although these verses are packed with great theological truths, let's limit our discussion to the one phrase, *in the fullness of time*, because this phrase actually speaks of the way in which the Father sent His Son. Before we actually turn to the study of the concept of the fullness of time, I'd like to lay just a bit of groundwork. Why did God wait so long to provide a way of salvation for all mankind if He had a plan all along? While I can't say that I have a real answer to that question, this verse helps us to understand that there was a specific season that the Father had in mind for His intervention in the human saga – a point in history when the times would have come to their fullness. Scriptures also indicate that He had this whole agenda orchestrated even before He created the earth. (Matthew 13:35, 25:34; John 17:24; Ephesians 1:4; Hebrews 4:3; I Peter 1:20; Revelation 13:8, 17:8)

When we look at the world condition at the time of Jesus, we see that so many factors came into perfect convergence at that one pinpoint in history. The Roman Empire, which ruled the world at that time, had imposed one political system throughout the civilized world – Pax Romana. This system allowed the countries under Rome's control to exercise a certain amount of autonomy as long as they did not violate the general authority of the empire. One of the provisions of Pax Romana was free passage between the individual cities, states, and regions under Roman rule. There were no visas or passports required as travelers made their way through the empire. In addition, the Romans built the most elaborate road system known up until that time. This extensive roadway system connected even the most remote parts of Africa, Asia, and Europe in a network so expansive that the proverb, "All roads lead to Rome," has endured to modern times. The superior quality of the construction technique of the Romans is evident today in roads and bridges that are still usable some twenty centuries later. I have personally ridden on two-thousand-year-old roads that are still in service in Israel and crossed a two-millennia-old bridge in Rome that today carries modern vehicular traffic safely from central Rome into the Vatican. God was waiting for the caesars to unify the nations and connect them with an outstanding transportation network, providing safe and dependable passage to the very ends of the world. Had He sent His Son before the rise of the Roman Empire, the possibility of the spread of the gospel to the far reaches of the globe would be hampered by lack of transportation and innumerable border restrictions. As it was,

24

the gospel was able to spread rapidly because the Roman Empire had eliminated almost all such hindrances.

When Alexander the Great died in a drunken stupor in 323 BC, he was lamenting that, at the age of thirty-three, there were no more worlds for him to conquer. No other military or political leader in all of human history has ever made such a claim or left such a legacy of bringing the total civilized world under the control of one individual in a single lifetime. As his armies swept their way around the Mediterranean and into regions of India and Africa, one deposit they left behind was the Greek language. Every territory that came under their power was required to adopt Alexander's tongue and become part of the unified language system he imposed. The genius of this language is that it is the most precise tongue ever spoken on the planet. With the intricate conjugation structure of the verbs and the elaborate declension system for the nouns, there is no question as to what a sentence is intended to say; the precise meaning of each statement is contained not only in the definitions of the specific words used but also in the forms in which those words are used. The Father used this uniquely fitted language to be the universal medium through which the message of His Son would be communicated. Even though Jesus did not personally speak the Greek language, those who recorded His sayings and documented His life took what they knew and communicated it with accuracy in Greek and then went forth to proclaim it in the one universally accepted tongue understood in all regions of the earth.

At the same time that Jesus was living on the planet, the entire world of religion was going through a state of flux. Even though Hinduism predates Christianity by almost a thousand years, it was in the same time frame that the Christian faith was spreading around the world that the Hindu religion was actually defining itself and codifying its teachings. Even though Siddhartha Gautama, the Buddha, lived some five hundred years before Jesus, it was only at the time of Christ that his teachings were being collected and organized. The religions of the Greeks and Romans were in the process of shifting from actual deity worship to a more philosophical interpretation as myth and legend rather than absolute factual interpretations. The Jewish faith, as it had existed for centuries, was also going through a major change so that the teachings of the rabbis, rather than the Old Testament scriptures, were actually becoming the measure of the faith. What the rabbis said about the scriptures became more authoritative than the scriptures themselves. It was at this exact period of history that such teachings were being recorded and preserved in the Talmud, Mishnah, and Midrash. God specifically timed the coming of His Son to be at a time when men all around the world from every form of religion were reevaluating what they really believed. Their hearts were ready and their souls were ripe for a new word from God – the Living Word. Both Jews and pagans were questioning what they had traditionally believed, and they were ready to respond quickly to the gospel. (Acts 6:7, 14:1, 19:27)

One other factor that figured into the rapid spread of the gospel is that God sent His Son just at the time of the great dispersion of the Jewish race from Israel. The Jews had already been scattered among all the nations of the earth to the point that the first century BC geographer Stabo said that there was no single place that had not received Jews. This spread of the race escalated with the Roman Empire's conquest of Palestine and the destruction of the city of Jerusalem in AD 70. At that time, the Jews were forcibly evicted in what has become known as the diaspora, or the dispersing of the race throughout the world. Because the Jewish faith and practice were essentially omnipresent, there was a ready platform upon which the Christian message could be presented around the world. Notice how the book of Acts repeatedly attests that the gospel was first introduced in the synagogues as it spread from city to city. (verses 13:14, 14:1, 16:13, 17:1, 17:10, 17:17, 18:4, 18:19, 18:26, 19:8, 22:19, 26:11) Paul clearly states that it was his deliberate plan of operation to go first to the Jewish community before moving to the gentiles. (Romans 1:16)

On another level, and likely the most important level,

the Father was waiting to send His Son at the precise moment in which the message would be recorded with the unique quality that makes the New Testament truly the Word of God. Because of the unique timing of the coming of Jesus, it was years after His life, death, and resurrection that the gospels were written down. There were several reasons why people, particularly the Jews, did not write their life stories during the period of the early church. First of all, not much of anything was written down at that time because most of the learning in this period was oral since most of the people were illiterate. First Corinthians 1:26-27 confirms that not many of the early Christian believers were educated. In fact, it is only in recent history that education has become widely accessible, a reality that Daniel spoke of as a sign of the last days. (verse 12:4) Secondly, Jewish scholars were cautious about writing down their teachings for fear that they would be considered to be attempting to equate themselves with the prophets and their work which was written in the Bible. The Jews said, "The last prophet was Malachi, and there are not any prophets in the world today." In addition, oral teaching was considered more noble than teaching communicated second-hand in written format. Scholars of the time said that the living voice was much richer. Memorizing and reciting the works of the ancients and the teachings of the contemporaries was considered an honorable activity. One of the contemporaries of Jesus boasted of having learned forty-eight books of Homer by memory. When a rabbi would give a teaching, the students would memorize it word-for-word. They memorized everything he was saying as he said it. After the class, two students would get together and quote the lessons back and forth to each other. If one of the students said one word differently from the way the other one remembered it, they would stop and discuss the point until they both came into agreement of exactly what that rabbi said word-for-word. Another reason that the gospels were not immediately written down was because printing was very expensive. Until the invention of the printing press some fourteen hundred years later, books had to be handwritten one at a time. At the time of Jesus, it cost twenty to twenty-five denarii to transcribe one hundred stichoi (about sixteen syllables). To get a perspective on what that meant, we can turn to the story that Jesus told in Matthew chapter twenty where vineyard workers earned a denarius for a day's wage. In other words, hiring a scribe was like hiring a highly skilled professional who got many times more than an average working man's daily wage. Another factor that kept the early Christians from recording the gospel stories immediately was their belief that Jesus was coming back in the Second Coming almost immediately. They took certain statements of Jesus such as Matthew 16:28 and Matthew 10:23 to mean that He would return so soon that there was not any reason to make copies of his story when they could just repeat the message by word of mouth. They felt that it was a better use of their time to go out and proclaim the message rather than to take the time to sit down and write it out.

However, within a few years, things began to change. The church realized that they needed reading material for their church services. The first-century church took its form of worship directly from the Jewish synagogue because most of the first-century Christians came from Jewish backgrounds. In the synagogue worship, one of the most important parts was the reading of the Torah, the Old Testament Law. Since the church followed the pattern of the Jewish ceremony, they needed a written part of the scriptures to read. They would read the Old Testament, but they also wanted the teachings of the apostles and of Jesus Himself. As early as 67 AD, Justin Martyr referred to reading the letters of the apostles for such church functions. There was also a missionary intent behind the writing down of the gospels. Try to read the gospels through as though you had never heard the stories before. Just sit down and read them like they are a new novel you just picked up at the bookstore. Do not think about all the sermons that you have heard about Jesus. As you read, you will become enthralled with the life of the Man. You will want to know more and more about Him. You will find that He always demands you to make a decision. You will either say, "This guy is a lunatic. He's absolutely crazy. He's berserk!" or you will decide, "These people are liars to make up such lies about such a man!" or you will say, "He has to be Lord." Out of the American Revolution grew the expression, "The pen is mightier than the sword." It was this same reality that drove the early believers to take the time to record this sharper-than-a-two-edged-sword message. Additionally, the church needed a source for catechetical teachings. The Old Testament leaders set up landmarks so children could ask questions and receive instruction. (Joshua 4:6) In the Jewish sedar service each Passover, the Jewish children always ask questions of the elders for the purpose of instruction, "Why is this night different from all other nights?" Christians realized that they needed a similar codified way of prompting children to learn about the faith of their fathers. The gospels were to be for answering the questions raised about Jesus. Heresy among adults was just as important a factor as was inquisitiveness among children. The gospels were to guard against heresy that was developing in relationship to the life story of Jesus. The pseudepigrapha, or imitation gospels that began to be circulated at this period, was full of examples of fantasy stories that soon began to be circulated as if they were the true gospel stories. One other motivating factor was the need to establish a direct link to the men who personally knew Jesus. (I John 1:1) The church needed to establish a direct chain with as few links as possible between Jesus and the existing church; therefore, the gospels were recorded by apostles who directly knew Jesus or disciples of these apostles.

The result of this lag in the production of the written gospels was that when the written product did appear, it was reflective history inspired by the Holy Spirit rather than historical documentation of news events. Some people perceive the inspiration of the Holy Spirit working in the gospel writers as though the authors were in a trance. Some view it like an instrument – as a man blowing a trumpet. These people believe that the gospel writers were like the trumpets and that they had nothing to do with what came out of them as the breath of God flowed through them. However, the inspiration was not of this nature as can be seen when we read through the different gospels. You'll see that there are different points and different influences in each book. This is because of the human nature of the person who was writing. The same Word of God was given by each writer, yet you can recognize characteristics of different personalities as they bring forth the message. The writers were writing about a historical event. They were the eyewitnesses who had seen it and experienced it, yet the Holy Spirit helped bring to their remembrance what went into the gospel at this point. (John 14:26) The Holy Spirit chose what was significant and gave the interpretation for it. To emphasize that one writer's personality shows up here or there does not in any way detract from the fact that the Holy Spirit inspired it. The Holy Spirit did inspire it. There are no errors in the gospels because everything was Holy Spirit inspired. But, because the gospels were not written the day after the events occurred, the accounts are not history in the sense of a newspaper report of an event. It is not like a television news reporter's on-the-spot news. It is a spiritual understanding of the event, written years later by men who have had time to reflect, and years for the Holy Spirit to quicken them to really know what that event was all about. If you think about something that happened to you years ago, you will only remember what that event was all about but not the minute details. God knew the exact moment in history to send His Son so that His story would be more than history; it would be the Word of God. The contemporary philosophy of oral, as opposed to written, teaching guaranteed that the gospel would not become a textbook history lesson, but a message of God's mercy reported after years of reflection in the writers' lives.

God sent His Son in the fullness of time when all aspects of politics, engineering, religion, and philosophy were totally lined up so that the message of the gospel would have the maximum impact in the shortest amount of time. Just as history was in the crosshairs when God sent His Son, Jesus sent His disciples out when all the conditions were exactly right for their success as well.

Two intriguing verses in the story of Jesus seem to focus on the concept that He entered human history at a very specific moment in time. In Luke 1:36, we read Gabriel's message to Mary concerning the conception of John the Baptist. He mentions Mary's cousin Elizabeth and says that she was called barren. Notice that he does not say that she was barren, only that people considered her so. The message behind the angel's wording is that there was a specific time at which John the Baptist was to be born. Since he was to be the forerunner of Jesus, he could not be born until it was almost time for Jesus to come on the scene. Therefore, Elizabeth had to wait until an advanced age to give birth to him. In other words, even though she was not barren, she could not give birth until the fullness of time. The other intriguing verse is John 4:4, where it is recorded that Jesus *must needs pass through Samaria* on His way from Judaea to the Galilee. The truth is that He actually didn't have to pass through Samaria at all. In fact, most Jews at this time in history had such animosity against the Samaritans that they avoided traveling through Samaria even though it was the most direct route between Judaea and the Galilee. They regularly traveled through the Jordan River Valley in order to bypass Samaria. Jesus could have easily followed this well-established route; however, there was something else at play in His decision that day. It was the fullness of time. There was a Samaritan woman who would be at the well at the exact time Jesus' journey would bring Him to that exact spot. The Father knew that she would be there and that she would be ready to hear what Jesus would have to say to her. He also knew that she would become a catalyst to bring revival to the whole city. Because of that, the Father compelled the Son to take that specific route at that specific time. Convergence was destined because it was the fullness of time for the woman at the well and for the city of Samaria.

When we are sent out to take part in the Great Commission, we can be assured that He is orchestrating everything in His precise timing; there is nothing that will happen by accident or random luck. When the football team is in the huddle, the quarterback may tell one of the runners to go down the sideline and turn around when he reaches the twenty-yard line. That's because he knows exactly what's in his mind for the next play. If the other player will only follow the quarterback's instructions, he will discover that just as he turns around at the twenty-yard line, the ball will be ready to fall into his arms. When it comes to the Great Commission, God has each play planned out in even more detail than the world's best quarterback. When He says that He's sending us, He has a doable plan in mind.

Evangelism

Since the point I want to stress at this juncture in the discussion is based on Mark's version of the Great Commission, it would be good to make a little side trip here to remove any questions you might have about that passage. Many modern versions of the Bible relegate the last few verses of Mark's gospel to the footnotes or even omit the section altogether. The reason for this is that several of the ancient manuscripts end with verse eight of chapter sixteen. Some biblical scholars argue that the original manuscript did, indeed, contain the disputed material but that it was somehow lost from one source that became the template for a number of copies that have survived until today. I have no problem with this explanation because I once had a Bible that was missing one of the books of Kings because the binding had broken and those pages simply fell out. I can easily imagine what would happen if I had been in a country where no other Bible was in circulation; the people would have accepted my Bible as the authority and made copies of it without the missing section. Other Bible scholars insist that the original document actually ended at verse eight even though this seems to be an abrupt and rather illogical way to end the gospel. In fact, a number of ancient documents contain endings that have been added to the text to bring it to a smoother and more logical ending. Scholars who hold that the original manuscript ended at verse eight view the ending found in the <u>King</u> <u>James</u> <u>Version</u> as just one of those proposed endings added by someone other than Mark. Even if we accept this theory, we must acknowledge that this ending is far more documented and accepted than any of the other possibilities. In answer to the question about the authenticity of the Great Commission passage in Mark, I would like to present a couple points for consideration. First of all, this ending has historically been accepted by the church. Even if it did not come from the hand of Mark, the church throughout the centuries has felt that it is enough in alignment with the rest of the gospel that they have not disputed or questioned it. The second point is that the ideas presented in the passage are confirmed in other parts of the scriptures, thus attesting to the validity of the content of the passage even if the passage itself is still held in question. Jesus' promise that believers would speak in tongues is fulfilled in at least three places in Acts (verses 2:4, 10:46, 19:6) and in the book of I Corinthians (chapters 12-14). His statement about laying hands on the sick for healing is validated numerous times in Acts (verses 5:12, 9:17, 14:3, 19:11, 28:8) and directly commanded in the book of James (verse 5:14). The statement about casting out devils is verified in Acts (verses 5:16, 8:7, 16:18, 19:15) and alluded to in Paul's epistles (Romans 8:15, I Corinthians 12:3, II Corinthians 11:4, Ephesians 2:2, II Thessalonians 2:2, I Timothy 4:1, II Timothy 1:7). The promise of divine protection from snakebites is illustrated in Paul's experience on the island of Melita in Acts 28. Hebrews 2:4 seems to be an all-inclusive statement which gives an across-the-board confirmation that God validated the ministry of the disciples through signs and wonders, miracles, and gifts of the Holy Spirit.

In the version of the Great Commission as it is recorded in the existing conclusion to Mark's gospel (verses 16:15-18), Jesus showed Himself to the eleven disciples who remained after Judas had turned traitor. As they gathered for a meal, He miraculously appeared to them with His directive. This encounter emphasizes the universal scope of the Commission coupled with the promise of supernatural authority to back up the message. If you don't mind, I'd like to take you on a bit of a journey to help unravel a few insights concerning this aspect of the Great Commission.

I'd like to begin by giving you a little tour of my family tree. One of my notable relatives is a cousin who has been the subject of a couple movies in that he masterminded one of the most daring jailbreaks in history by convincing his girlfriend to commandeer a helicopter and land it in the exercise yard at the state penitentiary where he was waiting to jump aboard and be whisked away to freedom. Another of my history-making relatives was a cousin five layers away who refused to surrender the Confederate cause simply because Robert E. Lee officially declared that the South was capitulating in the War Between the States. Manse Jolly continued to wage his own personal war for several years as the Union occupation forces were entrenched in his native South Carolina. Like a specter, he would appear from nowhere, charging through the camp on his trusty steed with a violent six-shooter in each hand. Before they knew what had hit them, he disappeared out the other side of the camp leaving behind a swath of death and injury. Hiding in wells, caves, forests, barns, and even – on one occasion – under the hooped skirt of a worshipper at a Sunday service in the local Baptist church, Manse continued to elude the entire US Army and all the scallywag bounty hunters even though the posters in all the post offices offered the largest bounty ever placed on the head of a fugitive at that point in history. I could entertain you for hours with stories of his one-man raids on the blue coat encampments and how he earned all the notches on his pistol handles. However, that's too far afield from today's topic. I simply introduced my cousin Manse because his story helps us understand the life of the prophet Jonah that I want to study in this section. One of the things that so incensed Manse Jolly was the Union's attempt to cripple the Southern states through what has become known as Sherman's March to the Sea. Like one gigantic razor, Major General William Tecumseh Sherman marched his troops through the Carolinas and Georgia, destroying everything in his path. More than a military campaign, this invasion was an attempt to bring not only the military forces of the Confederate States to their knees but to also demoralize and impoverish the general populace. Every plantation and farm house was burned, every cotton gin and grist mill was razed to its foundation, the crops were trampled, the fruit trees were uprooted, the cattle were slaughtered, the women were raped, the railroad tracks were ripped up and melted so that they could not be repositioned. In short, anything that could have possibly served to sustain not only the Rebel cause but the very existence of the residents was destroyed. As Sherman himself said, war is hell; but, for those people whose lives and livelihoods had gone up in smoke in the wake of Sherman's destruction, the flames of hell were a vivid reality as they languished in the devil's embers.

From my family tree, I'd like to make what might seem like an unusual leap to the prophet Jonah? The relationship between my cousin and the prophet is that the Assyrians had done exactly the same thing to the land of Israel that Sherman did to his Southern brothers. Isaiah 7:20 describes their invasion metaphorically as a razor shaving a man from his head to the very hair on his feet. It was to the capital of this evil nation that God asked Jonah to go. I can imagine that he harbored the same sentiment against the Assyrians that smoldered inside my cousin Manse toward the Yankees. I have little trouble imagining how quickly this disgruntled prophet packed his bags and rushed off in the opposite direction. When God finally got the prophet back on track and renewed His command to go prophesy in Nineveh, Jonah had just one consolation in the job he was pressed to do – he was commissioned to prophesy the city's imminent doom! I can imagine that even Cousin Manse would be willing to lay down his six-shooters if he could speak as the mouthpiece of God Himself declaring that the Yanks had only forty more days until they were to meet their demise. I wonder if Jonah's lips weren't curled up in a bit of a smile as he dished out the Doomsday message in the streets of Nineveh. Then, the unthinkable happened – the city repented. In the most dramatic revival ever chronicled, the entire city – including the animals – fasted and repented until God changed His mind about their destruction. For Jonah, this was just too much. He couldn't imagine how God could possibly betray him by allowing these undeserving aliens to live. Finally, God had to visit this evangelist (well, maybe that's not the best term since it means "one who preaches good news," and Jonah had brought a message of bad news) and explain to him His compassion for the hundred and twenty thousand humans plus a vast number of cattle (see, it did do some good for the cattle to fast along with the people).

Among many other truths that this story proclaims, there are several significant points concerning winning a city for Christ. The most obvious element of the story is the sheer magnitude of the revival: an entire city, from the king to the street sweeper – and even the cattle – turned to the Lord. As remarkable as the story of Nineveh's conversion is, it is not unique. The history of the Christian church is marked by many such revivals in which entire cities, countries, and people groups have responded to the gospel en mass. One such historic moment occurred in AD 723 when St. Boniface challenged the Germans to accept Christ. To prove that Jesus – not their pagan deity Thor – was the true god, the missionary took an axe and began to chop away at a mighty oak tree that the local people believed to be the dwelling place of their god of thunder and lightning. As the crowd cowered back expecting Thor to retaliate with a deadly bolt to defend his honor, Boniface continued to strike the tree until it came crashing to the ground. After this obvious validation of the Christian faith, the entire population converted and took the wood from the monstrous tree to build a chapel. During the first half of the sixteenth century, Francis Xavier turned entire communities in India and Japan to the Christian faith when he miraculously began to preach in their native tongues without ever having studied these languages.

More contemporary stories include a number of mass conversions that took place in the twentieth century. Following World War II, entire tribes of aboriginals in the Pacific islands turned to Christ when missionaries landed airplanes on their remote atolls. The story behind the conversions was that these islanders had never seen planes until they witnessed fighter planes flying over during the Pacific campaign. Many times, the pilots of these aircraft would jettison cargo that fell within reach of the natives. To them, these were gifts that the gods were dropping from the sky. When these heavenly visitations suddenly ceased, the tribal people had no idea that the war had ended; for that matter, they still did not even know that there was a war in progress. As they prayed for the gods to favor them with more visitations and more gifts, a cultish belief arose that the gods would someday return – an anticipation that they perceived as being fulfilled with the arrival of the missionaries. When the missionaries told them of Jesus, the people were primed for the message and readily received it. The account of the conversion of another entire tribal group centers around the introduction of a metal axe head to a Stone Age culture. When the courageous young missionary paddled the canoe containing his wife and two small children ashore in headhunter territory, the natives hid among the bushes determining the best time to stage their attack. As they lingered, the cannibals were amazed to see the gentleman fell a tree within minutes as he started to gather materials to build a home for his family. These primitive people, who had missed the advancements of the past three millennia, felt as if they had just witnessed a miracle since they were accustomed to spending hours and even days chopping down a tree with their stone axes. Their awe of this man's magical power led to respect for his message and acceptance of his God.

In the Solomon Islands, two young missionaries were captured by a bloodthirsty tribe and sentenced to death for trespassing on their territory. Since the king of the people happened to be seriously ill, the execution was postponed as the people focused all their energy and attention on the ailing monarch. When all the magical incantations of their shamans failed to revive the king, the missionaries were allowed to present their message before the chief and pray for him. Immediately after their prayers, the king died. As you might guess, this was not a plus for the evangelists. However, the king suddenly revived and sat up on his mat long enough to tell the people about his death experience and to confirm that what the missionaries had said was true. With the final admonition to his people that they should listen to and believe these foreigners, he fell back on his mat and died again. Instantly, the prisoners were released and welcomed among the people. Their message was heartily accepted and the entire populace became believers.

Two more accounts of massive revivals come from the

islands of the Philippines. A nation-changing movement swept the country after Dr. Lester Sumrall went into Bilibid Prison and cast the devil out of a young girl who was manifesting physical bite marks made by an unseen entity. She was literally being bitten by demons. Within six weeks, one hundred and fifty thousand conversions and innumerable healings were registered. It took weeks to baptize all the new believers. A more isolated example comes from a remote village where the resident witchdoctor challenged the newcomer missionary claiming that there could only be one spiritual leader in the area. He proposed a contest to see which one possessed more spiritual power, with the understanding that the one who failed the test would pack up and leave. A large stage was erected so that all the villagers could witness the match. The missionary, unsure as to how to proceed, invited the witchdoctor to go first. To her amazement, the witchdoctor lay down on the stage and began to levitate. Being considerably overweight, the missionary was sure that floating in the air was out of the question for her. When she questioned the Lord as to whether she should concede and start packing her bags to leave the village, the Lord impressed upon her that she was not to leave; instead, she was to prove her superior spiritual authority. Her very clear impression was that she should push the floating witchdoctor back to the ground; so, she gathered her skirt around her leg and raised her foot in order to plant her heel firmly in his belly. Taking advantage of her extra pounds, she slammed the floating witchdoctor to the floor and yelled to the spirit inside him to come out. Once the man was delivered, he immediately offered to leave town; however, the missionary persuaded him to stay, on the condition that he would accept Christ. Not only did he respond to her message, but the entire village also followed. The former witchdoctor became the mayor, and the missionary became the pastor, as the entire community became one large Christian neighborhood with everyone baptized members of the same church.

A little white-haired Indian man had been trying year after year to evangelize his remote village in Tamil Nadu state in southern India. Yet, his Hindu neighbors' hearts and ears were closed. Finally, one day at an evangelism training conference in the city of Madras (now known as Chennai), he learned the principles of the Great Commission that signs and wonders should accompany the proclamation of the kingdom. Returning to his village with a new power from his new relationship with the Holy Spirit, he found that an old lady in the village had been gored by a water buffalo. Laying his hands on her, he commanded that she be totally healed. Instantly, her crippled legs received strength and her mangled body was straightened. Since the whole village had seen the woman's condition after the attack and then saw her miraculous recovery, everyone suddenly believed that the old man's message was real. The village that had rejected his testimony year after year was converted overnight.

As we examine all these accounts, there is one major point that is consistent throughout – a miraculous catalyst to the revival. Even though the iron axe head and the airplanes were not supernatural, they certainly seemed so in the eyes of the primitive tribes who had never seen the "miracles" of modern technology. Although it is not mentioned in the biblical record, we must certainly assume that back in Nineveh, there was a definite impact when this shriveled-up, bleached-out prophet showed up. Having spent three days in the belly of the whale swishing around in gastric juices, he must have been something to behold! Certainly, the story of his history-making submarine journey accompanied, if not preceded, him. If this is indeed the case, there is no wonder that the king and all one hundred twenty thousand people in the city responded to his proclamation.

This is a consistent biblical pattern of evangelism. Miraculous acts at the hands of Daniel resulted in empire-wide decrees from the ruling monarchs themselves that the entire population must reverence the God of Daniel. (verses 4:1-37, 6:25-27) When Jesus sent His disciples out, He commanded them to accompany their proclamation of the kingdom with the demonstration of its presence, *Go preach saying, The kingdom* of heaven is at hand. *Heal the sick, cleanse the lepers, raise the dead, cast out devils: freely ye have received, freely give.* (Matthew 10:7-8) He added that even the citizens of Sodom would have repented had they been presented with a message confirmed with manifestations. (Matthew 10:15, 11:23-24; Mark 6:11; Luke 10:12) When He gave them the Great Commission, He ordered them to remain in Jerusalem until they were endued with the power of the Holy Spirit so that they would be able to confirm their message with signs and wonders. (Luke 24:49, Mark 16:17) The book of Acts records abundant examples of miraculous acts resulting in mass conversions: supernatural tongues on the day of Pentecost (verses 2:6-12), the healing of the lame man at the temple gate (verses 3:1-9), miraculous healings and deliverances in Samaria (verses 8:6-8), the raising of Dorcas from the dead (verses 9:39-42), an angelic visit to Cornelius (verses 10:1-8), and Paul's miraculous protection from a venomous snake bite and the healing of Publius' father on the island of Malta (verses 28:1-10). In fact, the Apostle Paul declared that having signs and wonders in conjunction with his preaching was his *modus operandi* and that this combination of miracle and message had allowed him to fully saturate his targeted region. *Through mighty signs and wonders, by the power of the Spirit of God; so that from Jerusalem, and round about unto Illyricum, I have fully preached the gospel of Christ…But now having no more place in these parts, and having a great desire these many years to come unto you.* (Romans 15:19-23) In his letter to the Corinthian church, he emphasized that he had come to them with the power of God as well as with God's powerful message. *And my speech and my preaching was not with enticing words of man's wisdom, but in demonstration of the Spirit and of power.* (I Corinthians 2:4) Perhaps his ministry in this particular city was particularly marked with miraculous signs and wonders because it followed immediately upon the heels of a rather unfruitful ministry in Athens where Paul seemed to rely on his human intellect and philosophical arguments rather than the miracle ministry which characterized his evangelism in other venues. (Acts 17:16-34)

Paul's Five Keys for Evangelism

The Apostle does not place all the credit for the effectiveness of his ministry on signs and wonders alone. In I Thessalonians 1:5, Paul makes one simple statement that reveals five distinct elements in his approach to winning a city – five keys to a city, if you wish to think of them as such.

For our gospel came not unto you in word only, but also in power, and in the Holy Ghost, and in much assurance; as ye know what manner of men we were among you for your sake.

The first key he mentioned was the Word. Here he is talking about the gospel message that has been confirmed and proven through the scriptures and then presented within a biblical context. The scripture is full of instruction to avoid various substitutes which can camouflage themselves as worthy ministry material but actually lead to confusion and disqualification of our ministries: philosophy (Colossians 2:8), vain deceit (Colossians 2:8), the traditions of men (Colossians 2:8), the rudiments of the world (Colossians 2:8), enticing words of man's wisdom (I Corinthians 2:4), profane and vain babblings (I Timothy 6:20, II Timothy 2:16), oppositions of science falsely so called (I Timothy 6:20), fables (I Timothy 1:4, II Timothy 4:4), vain jangling (I Timothy 1:6), Jewish fables (Titus 1:14), profane and old wives' fables (I Timothy 4:7), cunningly devised fables (II Peter 1:16), endless genealogies (I Timothy 1:4, Titus 3:9), foolish and unlearned questions (II Timothy 2:23, Titus 3:9), teachers having itching ears (II Timothy 4:3), teaching things which they ought not for filthy lucre's sake (Titus 1:11), strivings about the law (Titus 3:9), the commandments of men (Matthew 15:9, Mark 7:7, Colossians 2:22, Titus 1:14), the doctrines of men (Colossians 2:22), strange doctrines (Hebrews 13:9), and even doctrines of devils (I Timothy 4:1).

As has already been mentioned, it would be hard to define Jonah as an evangelist since he brought an oracle of destruction rather than a message of good news. However, we must recognize that the good message is not always a sweet message. In fact, the scriptures teach that the gospel is definitely confrontational and possibly even offensive. It is called a stone of stumbling, a rock of offence, and a stone upon which we can fall and be broken or which will fall upon us and grind us to powder. (I Peter 2:8, Matthew 21:44, Luke 20:18) Jonah certainly knew how to hurl that offensive stumbling stone into the pathway of his audience, but he was not alone. Paul described the situation in his day by saying that some preachers were filled with envy, strife, and contention as they preached; but, God used them anyway. (Philippians 1:15-18) In this regard, we must remember that Jesus described two very important elements in His parable about sowing seed – the seed and the soil into which it was sown. When He explained the parable, Jesus told us what the seed was and spelled out the significance of each of the four soils. Interestingly enough, He said nothing about the farmer who was sowing the seed. We have no idea at all about the motivation or technique of this farmer. All we know is that he sowed the seed. We must remember that the power of the seed is in the seed itself while the potential for productiveness is in the soil into which it is planted. Once the farmer releases the seed in this parable, he has no more control over its growth. Therefore, it is the gospel and the hearts of the hearers – not the preacher – that make the difference. Of course, this is not intended to negate the significance of the minister, only to emphasize the fact that God's Word can produce fruit regardless of the pipeline through which it is delivered. Just imagine how much more effective the ministry will be when the power of the Word and the receptiveness of the hearts of the recipients are coupled with a genuine sincerity and skill on the part of the preacher. Unlike Jonah, Paul had a true desire to see people saved and he made a deliberate attempt to relate the gospel to them in a way that they would find relevant and palatable. *To the weak became I as weak, that I might gain the weak: I am made all things to all men, that I might by all means save some.* (I

Corinthians 9:22) Like the Greeks with the Trojan horse and David at the watercourses of Jerusalem when he captured the city from the Jebusites (II Samuel 5:8), the Apostle looked for a way to get inside his target audience's defenses before he released his assault (I Corinthians 9:19-23). In many cases, his subjects didn't even know what had hit them until they were fully in the grasp of the gospel.

Paul's second key was power. All we need is a quick review of the book of Acts to see that his ministry was indeed accompanied with miraculous events just as we have seen in the previous chapter. (Acts 13:11, 16:16-18, 19:11, 20:9-10, 28:3-6) Next, Paul mentions the Holy Ghost. Since the operation of the gifts of the Spirit seems to have been his topic in the previous category, we must interpret this reference to suggest a fuller meaning of the operation of the Holy Spirit in the believer's life. Turning to his letter to the Galatians, we see at least two areas where the Holy Spirit's influence must be evidenced in a believer's life and ministry. The first is in chapter five verses sixteen and eighteen: walking in and being led by the Spirit. Such Holy Spirit orchestrated movement is not only vitally important to the success of our personal lives and the productivity of our ministries, but it may also mean the difference between life and death. As Paul mentioned in the Galatian passage, the fatally destructive works of the flesh will overcome us unless we walk in the Spirit. The Apostle was directed away from Asia toward a fertile ministry in Europe through the Holy Spirit's direction. (Acts 16:6-10) The inner voice of the Holy Spirit also warned Paul of the impending danger into which his ship was to sail. (Acts 27:10) The other Holy Spirit quality that Paul discusses in Galatians chapter five is the fruit of the Spirit listed in verses twenty-two and twenty-three. Just as no one cares for a barren tree that does not produce fruit (Matthew 21:19, Luke 13:6-7), people will not be attracted to our lives or ministries unless we manifest the fruit of the Spirit.

Paul follows with the quality of assurance. Even without an examination of some of the key biblical injunctions concerning assurance (Isaiah 32:17; Acts 17:31; Colossians 2:2; Hebrews 6:11, 10:22), we can recognize from the natural world that we never want to believe what someone is saying if we don't feel that he really believes it himself. I know that I'd never buy a car from a salesman if I saw him driving another make. Paul was persuaded of the validity of his message (Romans 8:38, 14:14; II Timothy 1:12) and admonished his disciples to be fully persuaded concerning their faith (Romans 14:5). Remember that Jesus promised that signs and wonders would follow the ministry of those who believe – not those who hope or wish. Assurance is the key to success in ministry.

Character is the fifth key that Paul used to open the city of Thessalonica to the gospel. In our Thessalonian passage, he called it his *manner of man*. To get a definition of this term, we can turn to his farewell to the Ephesian church where, again, he used this same expression and gave a rather lengthy explanation. The purity of his motives and the unselfishness of his service permeate the speech and testify to the quality of life he lived before the people. Who he was backed up what he said. As the old expression goes, he walked the walk as well as talked the talk. Another couplet reminds us that people don't care how much you know unless they know how much you care. Our personal character is likely the most powerful force in communicating to the city we wish to win for Christ. After all, many more people will read our lives than will ever read our tracts.

And when they were come to him, he said unto them, Ye know, from the first day that I came into Asia, after what manner I have been with you at all seasons, Serving the Lord with all humility of mind, and with many tears, and temptations, which befell me by the lying in wait of the Jews: And how I kept back nothing that was profitable unto you, but have shewed you, and have taught you publickly, and from house to house, testifying both to the Jews, and also to the Greeks, repentance toward God, and faith toward our Lord Jesus Christ...Wherefore I take you to record this day, that I am pure from the blood of all men. For I have not shunned to declare unto you all the counsel of God...Therefore watch, and remember, that by the space of three years I ceased not to warn every one night and day with tears...I have coveted no man's silver, or gold, or apparel. Yea, ye yourselves know, that these hands have ministered unto my necessities, and to them that were with me. (Acts 20:18-34)

Jonah's Missing Key

The next point I see in the story of Nineveh is the missed opportunity to shepherd the new converts. As best as we can tell, Jonah did nothing to follow up on the great revival in Nineveh. It was likely the greatest missed opportunity in all of human history; yet, Jonah had no concern for their spiritual needs. Had he built a church, he would have had one hundred percent of the population as members – and, more than likely, as tithers. Apparently, he had no interest in shepherding them and went back to his ordinary life. My point is that we need not only develop a strategy for winning people to Christ but also a strategy for keeping them once they have accepted the Lord. In other words, our evangelism must be followed with proper discipleship.

We can see an excellent example in the life of Paul – a man who was consumed with his love for the churches. Reading the introductions to his letters gives us a glimpse into his never-ending concern for the saints. To the Corinthians, he writes, *I thank my God <u>always</u> on your behalf.* (I Corinthians 1:4) To the Philippians, he says, *I thank my God upon <u>every</u> remembrance of you.* (verse 1:3) He addresses the Colossians, *We give thanks to God and the Father of our Lord Jesus Christ, praying <u>always</u> for you.* (verse 1:3) His greeting to the Thessalonian church reads, *We give thanks to God <u>always</u> for you all, making mention of you in our prayers.* (I Thessalonians 1:2) Timothy he addresses as *my own son in the faith* (I Timothy 1:2) and *my dearly beloved son* (II Timothy 1:2) and goes on to say, *I thank God, whom I serve from my forefathers with pure conscience, that <u>without</u> <u>ceasing</u> I have remembrance of thee in my prayers night and day.* (verse 1:3) Titus also receives the loving salutation of *mine own son after the common faith.* (verse 1:2) In writing to Philemon, Paul also addresses Apphia whom he called *beloved* (verse 2) and then writes, *I thank my God, making mention of thee <u>always</u> in my prayers.* (verse 4)

From these opening lines, we are able to get a glimpse inside the heart of a man capable of precipitating change in a city. His converts were never out of his heart and mind. No matter how many miles and how many years separated them, these loved ones were always in Paul's prayers. But, it is in his greeting to the church at Rome that we are able to really see what is in the heart of a true minister of God. Here, Paul is addressing a church that he has never visited and a congregation of believers who, except for a few individuals, were strangers to him. Yet, he confirms – and even calls upon God as his witness – that he is always and unceasingly interceding for them. This is a pastor's heart – a heart of unceasing love and concern for the Body of Christ, whether personal friends or total strangers. These believers he addresses as *beloved* and says,

> *I thank my God through Jesus Christ for you all, that your faith is spoken of throughout the whole world. For God is my witness, whom I serve with my spirit in the gospel of his Son, that <u>without</u> <u>ceasing</u> I make mention of you <u>always</u> in my prayers.*

In II Corinthians chapter eleven, Paul graphically illustrates how heavily the burden of love for the church weighed upon his heart. Here, he describes the physical difficulties he endured for the gospel's sake: beatings, imprisonments, shipwrecks, long journeys, plots against his life, attacks of wild beasts, assaults by robbers, hunger, exposure, and being stoned to the point of death. Yet, he concluded this list with, *Beside those things that are without, that which cometh upon me daily, the care of all the churches.* (verse 28) He seems to be saying that the inner burden he carried for the churches exceeded the physical burdens that had been hurled upon him externally. He wrote lengthy and detailed letters to minister to them, he went to great lengths to visit them and ensure their wellbeing (Acts 15:36), and he sent others in his place to guarantee that they had proper instruction and solid leadership in place (I Corinthians 4:17, Philippians

2:19, I Thessalonians 3:2, Titus 1:5). This is the heart of a man who will see fruit that remains long after the initial revival.

But, Paul is not our ultimate example. He was only outwardly manifesting the true life of Christ – the One who lived inside him. (Galatians 2:20) Luke 22:31 records that Jesus knew about Satan's plot to destroy Peter, so He prayed for him that he would not fall. In Matthew 23:37, we read that Jesus sat on the Mount of Olives and looked down on the city of Jerusalem with a heart that cried out for its people. He wanted to call them under His wings of protection, but they would not come to Him. It broke His heart because His was a true pastor's heart. The gospels continually repeat the theme that Jesus was moved with compassion for the people: the key to others' hearts and lives. When Jesus tried to illustrate what was in His heart, He used parables of a shepherd and his sheep. In Luke 15:4-7, He demonstrated that a shepherd is never satisfied until he has done everything possible to rescue every possible sheep.

What man of you, having an hundred sheep, if he lose one of them doth not leave the ninety and nine in the wilderness, and go after that which is lost, until he find it? And when he hath found it, he layeth it on his shoulders, rejoicing. And when he cometh home, he calleth together his friends and neighbors, saying unto them, Rejoice with me; for I have found my sheep which was lost. I say unto you, that likewise joy shall be in heaven over one sinner that repenteth, more than over ninety and nine just persons, which need no repentance.

The parable of the Good Shepherd from John 10:1-16 specifically speaks of Christ's love for the church, but it also illustrates the kind of heart that must be in any true minister through whom Christ's life is to be manifest.

Verily, verily, I say unto you, He that entereth not by the door into the sheepfold but climbeth up some other way, the same is a thief and a robber. But he that entereth in by the door is the shepherd of the sheep. To him the porter openeth; and the sheep hear his voice: and he calleth his own sheep by name, and leadeth them out. And when he putteth forth his own sheep, he goeth before them, and the sheep follow him: for they know his voice. And a stranger will they not follow, but will flee from him: for they know not the voice of strangers. This parable spake Jesus unto them: but they understood not what things they were which he spake unto them. Then said Jesus unto them again, Verily, verily, I say unto you, I am the door of the sheep. All that ever came before me are thieves and robbers: but the sheep did not hear them. I am the door: by me if any man enter in, he shall be saved, and shall go in and out, and find pasture. The thief cometh not, but for to steal, and to kill and to destroy: I am come that they might have life, and that they might have it more abundantly. I am the good shepherd: the good shepherd giveth his life for the sheep. But he that is an hireling fleeth, because he is an hireling, and careth not for the sheep. I am the good shepherd, and know my sheep, and am known of mine. As the Father knoweth me, even so know I the Father: and I lay down my life for the sheep. And other sheep I have, which are not of this fold: them also I must bring, and they shall hear my voice; and there shall be one fold, and one shepherd.

In John 21:15-17, the resurrected Lord confronted Simon Peter with the challenge that if he truly loved the Master, he would become a shepherd of the flock and *feed the sheep.* Peter apparently learned his lesson well and challenged others who wanted to become ministers in the Body of Christ to develop a shepherd's heart.

The elders which are among you I exhort, who am also an elder, and a witness of the sufferings of Christ, and also a partaker of the glory that shall be revealed: Feed the flock of God which is among you, taking the oversight thereof, not by constraint, but willingly; nor for filthy lucre, but of a ready mind; Neither as being lords over God's heritage, but being examples to the flock. And when the chief Shepherd shall appear, ye shall receive a crown of glory that fadeth not away. Likewise, ye younger, submit yourselves unto the elder. Yea, all of you be subject one to another, and be clothed with humility: for God resisteth the proud, and giveth grace to the humble. (I Peter 5:1-5)

In the words of both Jesus and Peter, a shepherd is not someone who holds the position for a paycheck. It has been my experience that those men and women who are really called into the ministry and have a desire to win their cities for Christ would almost be willing to pay to get to do their work. To them, their positions are ministries, not jobs. Thinking back to Jonah, we can see that he certainly did not have the heart of a true shepherd. His attitude was more precisely defined by the words of the prophet Jeremiah:

Woe be unto the pastors that destroy and scatter the sheep of my pasture! saith the LORD. Therefore thus saith the LORD God of Israel against the pastors that feed my people; Ye have scattered my flock, and driven them away, and have not visited them: behold, I will visit upon you the evil of your doings, saith the LORD. And I will gather the remnant of my flock out of all countries whither I have driven them, and will bring them again to their folds; and they shall be fruitful and increase. And I will set up shepherds over them which shall feed them: and they shall fear no more, nor be dismayed, neither shall they be lacking, saith the LORD. (verses 23:1-4)

In this remarkable passage, our God demonstrates His personal desire to see that the flock is shepherded. Our story of Jonah's evangelism in the Assyrian capital of Nineveh is marked by the unwillingness of the prophet to minister to the people and his utter dismay at the fact that God actually forgave these pagans. Unlike my cousin Manse and the prophet Jonah who wanted to draw small circles and leave certain individuals and entire ethnic groups outside, our God draws a huge circle that includes everyone. Second Peter 3:9 describes the heart of our heavenly Father this way, *The Lord is not slack concerning his promise, as some men count slackness; but is longsuffering to us-ward, not willing that any should perish, but that all should come to repentance.* From the first page of your Bible to its closing paragraphs, He is portrayed as an all-inclusive God. At least four times, the Lord reiterated that He intends to bless the entire human family through the descendants of His servant Abraham. (Genesis 18:18, 22:18, 26:4; Galatians 3:8) The Psalmist crafted a poetic prophecy affirming the all-inclusive nature of the Lord's love, *All the ends of the world shall remember and turn unto the LORD: and all the kindreds of the nations shall worship before thee.* (verse 22:27) The same sentiment was heralded by Isaiah at least twice during his prophetic ministry, *And it shall come to pass in the last days, that the mountain of the LORD'S house shall be established in the top of the mountains, and shall be exalted above the hills; and all nations shall flow unto it...This is the purpose that is purposed upon the whole earth: and this is the hand that is stretched out upon all the nations.* (verses 2:2, 14:26) According to Romans 11:26, the entire nation of Israel will eventually be saved. Two different prophets proclaim that the entire earth will be inundated with the glory of the Lord. (Isaiah 11:9, Habakkuk 2:14) The Old Testament declares and the New Testament confirms that it is the Lord's intent to pour out His Spirit on all flesh. (Joel 2:28, Acts 2:17) Jesus personally took His ministry to every city and then commissioned His followers to do likewise. (Luke 8:1-4, 10:1) He left no question in the minds of His followers that He intended that no one be excluded from receiving His message. (Matthew 24:14, 28:19; Mark 13:10, 16:15; Luke 24:47) The Apocalypse concludes with a futuristic insight into the time when this all-inclusive work will have been accomplished. (verses 7:9, 11:15, 21:24)

54

The story of Nineveh's conversion dramatically illustrates the paramount truth that God is much more interested in winning souls than we are. The Lord was so intent on saving Nineveh that He used a rebellious and disinterested prophet like Jonah to get the message out and to see that the job was done. If He got those overwhelming results from the unwilling prophet, just think what He might do through you and me if we are even casually concerned for the spiritual wellbeing of the lost souls of our world. Just imagine what can happen when we really get serious about our fellow citizens! There is no limit to the harvest we can reap if we are ignited with passion for the Great Commission.

My Journey into Discipleship

In Matthew chapter twenty-eight, Jesus appeared to the eleven on a mountainside in the Galilee area. There, He gave them a little different perspective on His Commission – discipleship.

And Jesus came and spake unto them, saying, All power is given unto me in heaven and in earth. Go ye therefore, and teach all nations, baptizing them in the name of the Father, and of the Son, and of the Holy Ghost: Teaching them to observe all things whatsoever I have commanded you: and, lo, I am with you alway, even unto the end of the world. Amen. (verses 18-20)

In order to unpack some of the principles of discipleship suggested in this passage, allow me to take you through my own spiritual pilgrimage since this verse is essentially my own personal calling.

As a child, I used to watch the *Jungle Book Adventures* on TV every Saturday morning. Hosting the program was a rotund, old fellow. Sitting in his favorite chair, he would reach for a volume of Rudyard Kipling's tales about India – the mystical, mysterious land of elephants, monkeys, tigers, and jungles. How I longed to step through the TV screen and find myself seated on top of one of those pachyderms! In my fascination with this wondrous land, I remember reading every word about India and every related topic in the World Book Encyclopedia. As my childish days gave way to maturity, the elephants and monkeys in my mind were replaced with knowledge of Shiva, Vishnu, Krishna, the caste system, the Atman, confusion, poverty, and despair.

As my understanding of what life is really about matured, I realized that what God had placed in my heart as a young child was not just wanderlust to see the world of *Jungle Book*, but a desire that matched the desire of His own heart – that all the world should know His Son Jesus. Any love for India on my part would have to be expressed in terms of my helping to bring the gospel of Jesus to the precious people of that part of the world. Then the Holy Spirit began to confirm my inner thoughts through prophetic words, sometimes from total strangers who had no way of knowing what was inside my heart and sometimes by Christian leaders whom I greatly respected and trusted, but all proclaiming the same thing: a global ministry. There were also dreams that widened my vision beyond *Jungle Book* as I saw myself ministering to people of all different colors, dressed in their native attire from all over the world. Yet, any actual participation on my part seemed less likely than my crawling through the television tube to join the *Jungle Book Adventures*.

Yet, as I mentioned, the desire that I had was only a reflection of the desire in God's own heart. Just as the moon doesn't have to be full of fire to produce light because it simply reflects the light emitted from the raging fire of the sun, I soon learned that I didn't have to generate the resources to fulfill the vision because all the resources were actually in the One with whom the vision originated. As I reflected His desire, He also provided the resources to make the vision possible.

Before long, I found myself traveling to country after country to share the good news of the gospel. But there was one thing that I noticed that was different about the ministry that God was leading me into. Instead of building dorms at orphanages or holding evangelistic rallies like almost every other missionary I would hear of was doing, I found myself teaching in churches, retreats, and conferences. In fact, it was somewhat of a running joke that every time I would get home from a mission, my pastor would ask me how many souls got saved, and I'd have to respond, "None." Then I'd have to remind him that I was speaking at a pastors' conference and that all the pastors were already believers.

One thing that I quickly recognized as I traveled through countries in Asia and Africa was that I had to adjust my teaching style in order to communicate fully with my audience. I soon found out that they didn't relate to messages about redemption and justification as readily as they did to the simple illustration of how an ugly caterpillar can become a beautiful butterfly. To them, the meaning of baptism was not found in Romans chapter six or Colossians chapter two; rather, it was in the simple stories of Jesus and John the Baptist on the shores of the Jordan or Philip and the eunuch at the pool in Gaza. The meaning of communion was not in I Corinthians, but in the Upper Room stories of the gospels.

At this point, allow me to share a little anecdote to illustrate what I discovered in those pastors' conferences. The guard at the border crossing was terribly perplexed by the little old man who pushed a wheelbarrow full of sawdust through the checkpoint each morning. Certain that the man was smuggling some contraband into the country, he searched the sawdust thoroughly each time the man came through. After weeks of futile searches, his curiosity and frustration overwhelmed him, and the guard finally promised not to arrest the old guy if he would only tell him what he was slipping across the border. The old man replied, "Wheelbarrows." What I discovered was that the vehicle I used to convey my message was actually the message itself. Therefore, I determined to use lots of illustrations as vehicles to convey my thoughts to the people. For example, I began to illustrate my message on how to receive the gifts of the Holy Spirit by tossing out candy to the audience. Because they had no problem receiving the free candy, it was easy for them to make the transition to understanding that they could also receive God's gifts just as freely. On one occasion, when I returned to the same area where I had used this illustration on my visit several years before, I was greeted as "the candy man" because of the impact of the illustration. Another sermon illustration I use to talk about the importance of what enters into our inner man through our eyes and ears and what comes out of our inner man through our mouths involves my Mister Potato Head toy that I have renamed as "Minister Potato Head." Wherever I use that illustration, I get repeated questions about my friend when I come back to the area – even years later. I discovered that illustrations don't have to be elaborate to be effective. When preaching about spiritual keys, I learned to simply pull my key ring out of my pocket and point to each key as I make the individual points. I learned to stop on the way into the church and pull a couple large leaves off a plant when ministering about Adam and Eve. For a lasting impression on the congregation, I would simply call up a couple from the audience to try to hide modestly behind these leaves. I discovered that messages about the armor of God were infinitely more effective if I brought in some army gear to hold up when I was talking. This may seem like a very simple point, but it made a world of difference in my ministry because I was beginning to move toward an important biblical teaching method: the use of illustrations demonstrated in so many of the Old Testament prophets (I Kings 11:30-40; II Kings 13:15-19; Isaiah 20:1-6; Jeremiah 13:1-11, 19:1, 25:15-36, 27:1-28, 43:6-13, 51:62-64; Ezekiel 3:2-3, 4:8-12, 5:1-17, 6:1-14, 12:1-16, 12:17-25, 24:1-27, 37:15-23; Hosea 1:1-11, 3:1-5) and the use of parables that dominated Jesus' ministry.

Because of the burning desire in my heart to help develop solid leadership for the churches in nations of the world where it was difficult to obtain a good Christian education, I began to work tirelessly recruiting students from third-world countries to attend the Bible college in America where I taught and also served as dean. Finding willing and qualified candidates wasn't a problem. The difficulties came with locating housing, finding scholarship funds, and raising living expenses for the students. It was a challenge, but I took it on because I really believed in the cause. Again, just as the sun provides all the illumination the moon needs, the Lord provided for these needs as well. Soon, our school blossomed into an international campus, with foreign students outnumbering the Americans. Unfortunately, there was a serious downside to the investment I was making.

60

These young African and Asian ministers became accustomed to living in American houses, driving American cars, and eating American food. Some even married American wives. And they weren't willing to give up these "luxuries" to go back home and minister in their own nations. It was then that I realized that there was something missing in the equation. Certainly, they were getting an excellent education and were being taught the "meat of the Word" as they sat under the instruction of some of the generation's greatest ministers. Yet, they were missing something. It was not content they lacked; rather, it was connection they were missing. Without a doubt, they were getting the best Bible curriculum available, taught by the most qualified instructors available; yet, somehow, they were failing to connect with the truth within the truths they were being taught. They were missing the lesson within their lessons, and they were not grasping the instruction in their instructors. As I faced disappointment after disappointment, I realized that the only solution was to train these developing leaders in their own environments so as to avoid the American distractions and allurements that could so easily deter, detain, detour, and derail them.

It was then that I understood the significance of the first word in the Great Commission – go. I could no longer expect the students to come to me if I was to accomplish what God had on His heart and had placed into my heart. I now realized that the dreams, visions, and prophecies of ministering to the nations meant more than simply training a few students from each nation and hoping that they would go back to their homes and impact their countries with what they learned in Bible school. Those visions, dreams, and prophetic words had to be taken literally that I was to go personally and take the gospel to them. With that revelation, I began to organize my life for transition. Knowing that I would have to leave my full-time position at the Bible college, I began to get my finances and family arrangements in line for the "move" – one that I assumed would be a logical transition to the *Jungle Book* mission field of Nepal.

As a Hindu kingdom in the Himalayas, Nepal had been a closed country where Christian ministry was forbidden and conversion to the Christian faith was a criminal act. I had been heavily focusing my prayers toward that nation for several years, asking the Lord to turn the heart of the king as He had promised in Proverbs 21:1. Then suddenly in 1990, with one stroke of the pen, Birendra Bir Bikram Shah Dev granted religious freedom to the people. I immediately began going into Nepal to help train and equip the emerging Christian leadership. Being one of the first international ministers to come to the country after this new freedom, I was able to make grassroots connections and to "get in on the ground floor," as the expression would go. One area of involvement that the Lord directed my wife and me into was the building of a Bible school to train the upcoming leadership. With this school in place, it seemed only natural that my next step in fulfilling the destiny to which God had called me would be to move to Nepal to oversee the school. With so many years' experience in teaching in and directing a Bible school, it seemed like a natural next step both for me and for the college in Nepal.

However, God is not interested in natural next steps; He is always working in the supernatural rather than the natural, and He often makes quantum leaps rather than next steps. Every time I would pray about making my move, the Lord would direct me to read Matthew 28:19, *Go ye therefore, and teach all nations* I would respond, "Yes, Lord, I'm ready to go to Nepal and teach. You just show me when." He would then respond, "You haven't read Matthew 28:19." I would argue back that I had read it and that I was ready to go to Nepal as soon as He would release me to go. Again, the Lord would challenge me that I hadn't read the passage, and, again, I would argue. Finally, one day I saw it – the passage said *all nations*, not "Nepal." At that point, I remembered the one common thread that ran through all the dreams, visions, and prophecies I had received: I had to go to the nations all around the globe! Finally, I was beginning to grasp the meaning of another element in the Great Commission – all nations.

This new comprehension of what God wanted to do in, through, and for me – and any and every willing member of His Body – took me through three levels of thinking: individuals, nations, all nations. First, I had to understand that the focus had to shift from individuals to nations. Of course, everything that God does, He does through individuals. If we read through the New Testament, we see that there was always a key person who was reached as the gospel spread into any new area. The woman at the well opened up the whole of Samaria to the good news. Lydia was the connection for the gospel in Macedonia. Aquila and Priscilla were the prime movers in Corinth. Publius was the catalyst for the message to be received on Malta. But notice how little attention is actually given to these individuals in comparison to the weight of the story dedicated to the city, region, or nation they impacted. On the other hand, these individuals are not just faceless statistics. They and the roles they played are significant enough that their names are recorded for posterity and they seem personable enough that we feel a true flesh-and-blood connection with them even millennia later. The scriptures in no way discount the ministry to individuals; however, it is evident that God's ultimate goal and the focus of His attention are upon eventually impacting the nation as a whole. Think of the stories that you've known since Sunday School: a young boy named Joseph was sold as a slave, yet he saved the whole nation of Egypt; one man named Daniel went into a den of lions, yet his testimony was published through all the provinces of Babylon; one young lady won a beauty contest, yet she turned the entire destiny of Persia; one queen was stirred by the report of Solomon's wealth and wisdom, yet she brought back the message to the entire nation of Sheba – and the list goes on and on.

What's even more intriguing is that the scriptures confirm repeatedly that God not only deals with nations as a whole; but, His true desire is for all nations – not isolated individuals within a nation or pockets of individuals within that nation, or even for a whole nation itself. Here is the next paradigm shift: from individuals to a whole nation and then from a nation to all the nations of the world. God wants all nations, and He repeatedly confirms it in His Word from Genesis to the Apocalypse.

Although we know Abraham as the father of the Jews, it would be good for us to revisit his story and take a look at the encounter with God in which he actually received the covenant that set him apart from other humans as God's special man.

And I will make of thee a great nation, and I will bless thee, and make thy name great; and thou shalt be a blessing: And I will bless them that bless thee, and curse him that curseth thee: and in thee shall all families of the earth be blessed. (Genesis 12:2-3)

The end result of God's calling upon Abraham and his descendants was that all the families of the human race would eventually be blessed because of their special covenant relationship with God. The New Testament confirmed this truth when the Apostle Paul was inspired to pen Galatians 3:8 where he defined the families spoken of in Genesis as all the nations of the earth.

Interestingly enough, Israel is repeatedly seen in the scriptures as being of special note among all the nations of the earth – sometimes, in a positive light, and, sometimes, in a very negative light. When Israel was obedient and blessed, all the nations were drawn to it because of its unusual prosperity; but, when Israel sinned against God, He scattered its people among all the nations of the earth, not just as judgment through removing them from their Promised Land but also as a way of giving the nations of the earth total exposure to these unique people of God. (Amos 9:9) Even when Israel was in rebellion against God and He had withdrawn His hand of blessing from them, the people of Israel were still a focal point of attention among all the nations of the earth because of the unusual calamity of such a prominent nation having come to such ruin.

(Deuteronomy 26:19, 28:1, 28:37, 29:24; I Kings 4:31; I Chronicles 14:17, 16:24; II Chronicles 7:20, 32:23; Malachi 3:12) The ultimate goal of this curious fascination with this one nation is that all the nations of the earth would come to recognize the God of the people as well as the people of God. (Psalm 67:2, 72:11, 72:17) Jesus would later say of the church that we are the light and salt of the world (Matthew 5:13-16); but, at this time Israel was like a candle on a candlestick when they were showing forth God's blessings and like salt scattered among the nations when they were under judgment.

With the advent of the church, the mandate of proclaiming the universal message to all nations was entrusted to these new representatives. (Matthew 24:14, 28:19; Mark 13:10; Luke 24:47; Romans 16:26) However, in His grace, God made the mandate of the church's expose' to the nations contingent upon their willingness to go voluntarily to the nations as opposed to the scattering He did with the disobedient Jews. Other than the one example given in Acts 8:1 where it seems that the persecution in Jerusalem precipitated the migration of the Christians, the gospel was spread by those who willingly surrendered to the Great Commission's mandate to go into all the world with the divine message. Even in the case of the Apostle Paul who was taken as a prisoner to Rome, he made the volitional decision to go to Jerusalem, knowing that the end result would be his arrest. (Acts 21:13) He also exercised his right as a Roman citizen to be taken to Rome for trial rather than to subject himself to extradition to Jerusalem. (Acts 25:11)

It is only logical that God would be motivated to capture the attention of entire nations at a time and to ultimately motivate all nations together. Even though He is the God of all nations (Psalm 82:8, 86:9, 113:4), God's archenemy has a plot to corrupt, pollute, and, therefore, destroy all these nations (Habakkuk 2:5; Revelation 14:8, 18:3, 18:23). Even though this diabolical plot has left all nations in line for the judgmental wrath of God (Isaiah 34:2, 40:17; Jeremiah 30:11; Joel 3:2; Zechariah 14:2, 14:19; Matthew 25:32; Revelation

12:5), God has an ultimate plan to bring all nations to redemption and grace (Isaiah 2:2, 25:7, 66:18, 66:20; Jeremiah 27:7; Revelation 7:9, 15:4).

The scriptures declare that God deals sovereignly with all nations (Acts 14:16, Romans 1:5) and that He ultimately sees all nations as equal and the same (Acts 17:26). God foreshadowed His plan of redemption for all nations under the old covenant by declaring that the temple in Jerusalem was not just a house of worship for the Jewish people, but that it was a house of prayer for all nations. (Isaiah 56:7, Mark 11:17) When speaking of the coming of Jesus, He was not simply seen as the messiah for the Jews but as the very desire of all the nations. (Haggai 2:7)

But, let's get back to the story for now. Dr. Lester Sumrall used to say that there are three stages of life. He said that the first thirty years of a man's life are for learning, the middle thirty years are for using what you have learned, and the final thirty years are for sharing all that you've learned through education and experience. I remember meditating on his words on my sixtieth birthday, reevaluating my first two thirty-year segments and wondering what the final phase would hold. Certainly, the first thirty years had been filled with learning – school, university, graduate school, and seminary. Interestingly enough, I had taken my position as dean of World Harvest Bible College when I was thirty years old as I was moving into those years when I was to use all that I had learned. For those next thirty years, I taught and administered in the school and church and eventually made a transition to a new chapter in my life in Colorado Springs. In Colorado, I took a part-time position teaching in a Bible school while focusing on doing mission work and getting into print a long list of books I had been working on during my career years. But, still the question loomed in my mind as to how the final phase would be different from those middle thirty years I had spent as a teacher – was that not the sharing stage? It was only at the end of the sixty-first year that I was able to look back and realize that I had actually published seventeen books and

66

Peggy had published her first book since our sixtieth birthdays. In addition, Peggy and I had entered into a new dimension of ministry of leading teams of Bible college students on mission trips to share with them what we have learned from our years of mission work. I had also been given the privilege of helping develop a whole new discipleship curriculum to be used by Every Home for Christ in their ministry around the world. One "chance meeting" thrust me into the sharing stage of my life and the final phase of the mission of discipling all nations.

It all began with a "bad hair day" that made us late for church one Sunday morning. As Peggy and I slipped into the sanctuary a bit tardy, our regular seats four rows in front of the sound booth in section one were already taken; so, we wound up finding a spot in the back of the auditorium. A little later, two more latecomers took the empty seats in the row in front of us. These stragglers were Dick Eastman, the President of Every Home for Christ, and his wife Dee. Later in the service, we had a chance to meet them, and we eventually asked them to join us for lunch. They graciously accepted our invitation and met us at a nearby restaurant where we shared about our connection with Every Home for Christ in Nepal. When Dick asked about our ministry, we told him about our call to go to developing nations and train the Christian leaders in some of the truths we had spent the last twenty-five years teaching in the Bible schools here in America. Immediately, he had his electronic organizer out of his pocket and was typing in our phone number and email address. Within a couple days, one of his top staff members contacted me and asked to set up a meeting. That meeting led to another and eventually to the request that I assist Every Home for Christ in a project that they were just initiating – a program for training Christian leaders in developing nations! We were late for church and not in our right seats, but we were in the right place at the right time to meet the right man just when he needed our help! The outcome of this divine appointment was a worldwide platform for helping to develop and launch a discipleship curriculum based on all the Great Commission principles I had begun to understand as I had journeyed beyond *Jungle Book*. I became part of an international team who was developing a discipleship method that we decided to name Be Fruitful and Multiply because we genuinely believe that the focus on studying the Bible itself will produce fruit in the lives of the believers and the discovery process where the individual is allowed to find truths for himself, rather than to have the principles handed to him by others, will produce such excitement that the new convert can't help but share his revelations with others.

A Fresh Look at Discipleship

Now, let's go back to the discussion I was having with God over the Great Commission passage in Matthew's gospel. Although I was very familiar with the <u>King</u> <u>James</u> <u>Version</u>'s rendering, to *teach all nations*, I was also aware that most modern translations use the wording *make disciples of all (the) nations* (<u>Bible</u> <u>in</u> <u>Basic</u> <u>English</u>, <u>American</u> <u>Standard</u> <u>Version</u>, <u>Montgomery's</u> <u>New</u> <u>Testament</u>, <u>Darby's</u> <u>Translation</u>, <u>New</u> <u>King</u> <u>James</u> <u>Version</u>, <u>Revised</u> <u>Standard</u> <u>Version</u>, <u>World</u> <u>English</u> <u>Bible</u>, <u>Twentieth</u> <u>Century</u> <u>New</u> <u>Testament</u>, <u>Weymouth's</u> <u>New</u> <u>Testament</u>) or simply *disciple all the nations* (<u>Young's</u> <u>Literal</u> <u>Translation</u>). Earlier, I expressed concern about the fact that we have felt that discipleship had to be relegated to a specifically trained group of teachers or trainers. In trying to unravel what Jesus meant by His directive to disciple the nations, I felt that I should check to see if there were any specific truths I might discover by investigating the Greek word used in the text. The first thing I found was that the word is used very sparingly in the verbal form in the New Testament. In fact, it is found only three other times in addition to Matthew 28:19. In Matthew 13:52, the verb is used to speak of a scribe who has been so well instructed concerning the kingdom of heaven that he is able to bring forth out of the treasury of his knowledge things new and old – things that were taught to him and things that he perceived on his own. In Matthew 27:57, the term is used to describe Joseph of Arimathaea who was so well taught concerning Jesus that he was willing to jeopardize his position on the Sanhedrin Council by siding with the man they were executing and to give up his valuable tomb for a man considered a criminal by the leading authorities of the time. In Acts 14:21, the word is used to describe the instruction that Paul gave to the believers in Lystra. Apparently, he was only there for a short period, yet the foundation he laid was sufficient to sustain the believers and proved to be the seedbed out of which sprang Paul's great protégé, Timothy.

The limited references to the verb didn't reveal much about the actual process itself; rather, it revealed more about the end result of having been through the process. The obvious end product of the process was a believer who was well grounded in his faith and understood it well enough to give his own insights rather than to just repeat the teachings of his instructor. Those individuals who were described as having gone through this process were solid and unshakable in their conviction and dedication to their faith. Joseph of Arimathaea, for example, was willing to put everything on the line – his present position and his eternal destiny – because of what had been instilled in him through this process of discipleship. Those individuals at Lystra who went through even a short version of this discipleship process were not only stable believers but also reproducing believers who were able to pass on their faith to a new generation in such young trainees as Timothy.

Ironically, through studying the verb, I learned more about those individuals who have been through the process than I did about the process itself, and I learned much more about the process itself by studying the passages that use the noun that refers to those who have been through the process. The first thing that I learned was that the process involves a strong personal commitment between the master and the disciple. As I read the story of Jesus and His disciples, I saw that they essentially lived together – traveling from place to place together, sharing meals, and living through personal traumas and even squabbles together. The next thing that became obvious was that the discipleship relationship is expected to be the highest commitment in the life of the person going through the process. Jesus described this dedication: *If any man come to me, and hate not his father, and mother, and wife, and children, and brethren, and sisters, yea, and his own life also, he cannot be my disciple.* (Luke 14:26) *And whosoever doth not bear his cross, and come after me, cannot be my disciple.* (Luke 14:27) *So likewise, whosoever he be of you that forsaketh not all that he hath, he cannot be my*

70

disciple. (Luke 14:33)

One of the aspects of the discipleship process that I found most intriguing was the apparent teaching method Jesus used with His disciples. Let's join in with Jesus and His disciples on the day He shared with them the Parable of the Sower:

> *And the disciples came, and said unto him, Why speakest thou unto them in parables? He answered and said unto them, Because it is given unto you to know the mysteries of the kingdom of heaven, but to them it is not given. For whosoever hath, to him shall be given, and he shall have more abundance: but whosoever hath not, from him shall be taken away even that he hath. Therefore speak I to them in parables: because they seeing see not; and hearing they hear not, neither do they understand. And in them is fulfilled the prophecy of Esaias, which saith, By hearing ye shall hear, and shall not understand; and seeing ye shall see, and shall not perceive: For this people's heart is waxed gross, and their ears are dull of hearing, and their eyes they have closed; lest at any time they should see with their eyes, and hear with their ears, and should understand with their heart, and should be converted, and I should heal them. But blessed are your eyes, for they see: and your ears, for they hear. For verily I say unto you, That many prophets and righteous men have desired to see those things which ye see, and have not seen them; and to hear those things which ye hear, and have not heard them. Hear ye therefore the parable of the sower.* (Matthew 13:10-18)

From this passage, it becomes apparent that Jesus chose to speak to His disciples in story form in order to separate those who had a real heart for the gospel from those who didn't have that genuine inner hunger for the truth. Choosing not to give facts and figures that everyone could understand, Jesus related stories with intrinsic messages and symbolism. For those who already had the kingdom of God inside them, the hidden meaning about the kingdom was readily awakened when they heard the stories. To those without the kingdom of God inside them, the message remained alien. Evidently, the high level of commitment that Jesus demanded from those who would be His disciples and the intertwining of their lives proved that these chosen ones genuinely had the kingdom already inside them and that they could, therefore, comprehend the essence of the story.

In Mark's account of the story, Jesus used some especially revealing wording when talking with His disciples about the use of parables, *And he said unto them, Know ye not this parable? and how then will ye know all parables?* (verse 4:13) When He asked if they knew the story, He used the term *eido*, which comes from the root word for "to see," suggesting that the disciples should have the revelation or insight about the parable; but, when He asked how they planned to know all other parables, He switched to the term *ginosko*, meaning to understand through experience. When Jesus had the discussion with the disciples as to why He continually used parables, He said that the ability or privilege to know the mysteries of the kingdom of God had been given to them, using the term *ginosko*, referring to understanding through experience. Yet, when He spoke of the outsiders, He used the term *suniemi*, referring to understanding that comes from putting the pieces together. In other words, if you are already experiencing the kingdom of God, you'll have insight into what the parables are communicating; if the kingdom of God is not already inside of you, you'll not be able to put the puzzle together to see the full picture.

At this point, the picture begins to crystalize that the discipleship process is not so much a teaching of doctrine as it is an awakening of what God has already placed inside the disciple. With this thought in mind, let's look at how Jesus taught His disciples to go about spreading the gospel:

After these things the Lord appointed other seventy also, and sent them two and two before his face into every city and place, whither he himself would come. Therefore said he unto them, The harvest truly is great, but the labourers are few: pray ye therefore the Lord of the harvest, that he would send forth labourers into his harvest. Go your ways: behold, I send you forth as lambs among wolves. Carry neither purse, nor scrip, nor shoes: and salute no man by the way. And into whatsoever house ye enter, first say, Peace be to this house. And if the son of peace be there, your peace shall rest upon it: if not, it shall turn to you again. And in the same house remain, eating and drinking such things as they give: for the labourer is worthy of his hire. Go not from house to house.
(Luke 10:1-7)

Notice that the passage we so often quote in the context of raising up missionaries and evangelists, *The harvest truly is great, but the labourers are few: pray ye therefore the Lord of the harvest, that he would send forth labourers into his harvest,* is right in the center of His directive for the disciples to go out on their mission. He was not sending them to the churches where they could recruit evangelists and missionaries, but to places where He had not yet been – to the mission field itself. Perhaps we have too often isolated this message from its context and have, therefore, missed the major emphasis of Jesus' words. As the disciples were to go out to minister, they were directed to be in constant prayer for someone else to be raised up to continue the ministry. The disciples were not to go out with the anticipation of bringing in the harvest singlehandedly; rather, they were to go out with the anticipation of seeing other harvesters raised up. In other words, they were to expect that they would duplicate themselves through their mission. Next, they were not to anticipate bringing in huge harvests as much as they were to look for some specific individuals whom Jesus labeled as the sons of peace in each community. Once they found these specific individuals, they were to enter into their homes and not wander around the neighborhood. In essence, they were to settle in on one individual household and invest in that home the way Jesus had invested in them – eating, sleeping, working, playing, laughing, and crying with them – until the knowledge of the kingdom of God that was inside those individuals was brought to full fruition. I'm certain that this approach did not preclude them from doing mass evangelism any more than Jesus had to give up ministering to the multitudes in order to disciple His chosen twelve. If we look into the life of Paul, we see this pattern at work when he focused on Lydia's household while ministering to the whole city of Philippi and when he joined Aquila and Priscilla in their tent making business while ministering to the whole city of Corinth. When Paul entered Corinth, the Lord spoke to him that He had *much people* in the city. (Acts 18:10) This revelation came before the city was evangelized, indicating that there were many sons and daughters of peace in the city, waiting to be revealed.

Notice how Paul so focused on his relationship with certain individuals that he essentially adopted them as his own spiritual sons: Timothy (Philippians 2:19-22, I Timothy 1:2, II Timothy 2:1), Titus (Titus 1:4), and Onesimus (Philemon 1:10). Peter also had this same kind of intimate relationship with John Mark. (I Peter 5:13)

Before we jump too quickly at some "New Age"y idea about waking "the god within," let's take just a minute to look at a couple passages from the scripture to get a clear biblical perspective. In Romans chapter one, Paul explained that he was not ashamed of the gospel because he understood how it could bring salvation to those who would walk by faith and that God actually revealed Himself more clearly to those who exercised their faith as they moved from one level of faith to the next. He then added a sad explanatory note that people would choose not to walk by this faith and would, therefore, reject the gospel and become increasingly aware of the judgmental wrath of God rather than His righteous grace.

For I am not ashamed of the gospel of Christ: for it is the power of God unto salvation to every one that believeth; to the Jew first, and also to the Greek. For therein is the righteousness of God revealed from faith to faith: as it is written, The just shall live by faith. For the wrath of God is revealed from heaven against all ungodliness and unrighteousness of men, who hold the truth in unrighteousness; Because that which may be known of God is manifest in them; for God hath shewed it unto them. For the invisible things of him from the creation of the world are clearly seen, being understood by the things that are made, even his eternal power and Godhead; so that they are without excuse: Because that, when they knew God, they glorified him not as God, neither were thankful; but became vain in their imaginations, and their foolish heart was darkened. (verses 16-21)

Later in the same book, Paul slipped in one little thought that can help us get a clearer understanding of the dynamic of what he was explaining in chapter one. In verse three of chapter twelve, he explained, *God hath dealt to every man the measure of faith.* Every man has an initial deposit of faith; therefore, every man is susceptible to the gospel. However, if it is only those who decide to walk by that faith who will receive the revelation of the righteousness of God, then it would be only those who could be classified as "sons of peace" – the Lydias, Aquilas, and Priscillas in the nations we are to disciple.

From these passages, we are able to gather some insight into how Jesus intended for us to disciple the nations. Our first focus should be to find a son or daughter of peace in the area and begin to invest our lives in that individual and his or her family. The biblical example was to essentially move in with the family. In most cultures today, this would not be practical; however, we need to make ourselves totally available and totally vulnerable to this son or daughter of peace and his or her family. Essentially, we are to instill into them who we are, as much as what we believe. Paul wrote of Timothy, saying that he had fully known his doctrine and his manner of life. (II

Timothy 3:10) Raising up believers is not just a matter of teaching them what we know, but also letting them know what we are. The end goal would be that we could say to them as Jesus said to His disciples, *He that hath seen me hath seen the Father.* (John 14:9) Perhaps this is what Jesus intended when He told the disciples that they would <u>be</u> <u>witnesses</u> (Luke 24:48, Acts 1:8) rather than sending them out to <u>do</u> <u>witnessing</u>. At the same time, we should continue to evangelize among the general populace, hoping to encounter even more sons and daughters of peace. In both of Luke's accounts of the Great Commission – one found in his gospel and one recorded in the book of Acts – the idea that Christians are to be witnesses is found.

> *And ye are witnesses of these things. (Luke 24:48)*
> *But ye shall receive power, after that the Holy Ghost is come upon you: and ye shall be witnesses unto me both in Jerusalem, and in all Judaea, and in Samaria, and unto the uttermost part of the earth.* (Acts 1:8)

Matthew 24:14 confirms that this witness element of the gospel will go throughout the whole world before the Lord's return.

> *And this gospel of the kingdom shall be preached in all the world for a witness unto all nations; and then shall the end come.*

The interesting point here is that we are called to give reports of what we have experienced just as a witness in a court case is called upon to tell what he has seen or heard. The important point is that we don't confuse our role with that of the Holy Spirit. We are witnesses, simply telling what we have experienced firsthand. (I John 1:1-3) Our role is not to convince anyone to believe or accept what we are testifying about. It is the work of the Holy Spirit as the attorney to convict and convince them to believe and respond to our testimony. Jesus said that the Holy Spirit would reprove the world of sin, righteousness, and judgment (John 16:8), using a

Greek word that literally means to cross-examine. In a court of law, the attorneys have the role of asking questions of the witnesses to prompt them to give testimony as evidence that they (the attorneys) can later use when presenting their cases. This is the interaction of the roles of believers and the Holy Spirit. He prompts us to tell things from our own experience, and then He works in the hearts of the listeners to make our testimonies affect their lives. It is through this process that we are able to engage the sons and daughters of peace that we encounter.

Sons and daughters of peace are often exactly the ones we would expect. For example, Barnabas – even though we really never meet him prior to his conversion to Christ – seems to be exactly the kind of person we (and, hopefully, God) would choose as our representative. He was from a religious background (Acts 4:36), he was generous (Acts 4:37), he was willing to go out of his way to use any influence he had to help others (Acts 9:27), and he was levelheaded enough to be willing to meet and discuss issues with those of differing opinions even though he was unmovable in his convictions (Acts 15:2). Even when he had to stand his ground so firmly as to part ways with Paul, he was gracious enough to take John Mark under his wing and nurture him to the point that Paul eventually asked for him to be brought back to him (Acts 15:36-41, II Timothy 4:11). One major quality of sons and daughters of peace is faithfulness, a quality that is repeatedly mentioned in the context of discipleship. (Matthew 25:21, 25:23; Luke 19:17; II Timothy 2:2; Titus 1:5-16; Revelation 17:11)

On the other hand, we see one startling truth about the son-of-peace concept in the life of the Apostle Paul. Sometimes, the son of peace will actually turn out to be the most unlikely candidate. Saul of Tarsus, who was *breathing out threatenings and slaughter against the disciples of the Lord* (Acts 9:1), would certainly not have been my most likely choice for the son of peace who was to bring the gospel – not to just one city or nation, but to the whole Gentile world and multitudes of Jewish background as well. It was his dramatic encounter on the road to Damascus that turned his life around, but I suspect that there had been a long process in his life that actually led up to this encounter. We can find a number of clues in his testimony that indicate that the kingdom of God was already inside of him just looking for a way to get out.

First of all, we see that Paul was interested in theology. He grew up as a freeborn Roman citizen (Acts 22:28) in the city of Tarsus, which he called *no mean city*, indicating that it was far above the average city of his time (Acts 21:39). Indeed, it was a major center of commerce, education, and military power. With the excellent education evidenced by the quality of his writings, his Roman citizenship with all its privileges, plus the strong ethic his Jewish upbringing afforded him, Paul would have been a success in any field he chose to pursue: business, military, academics, etc. Yet, he chose to abandon all of those lucrative possibilities and give himself to the study of theology at the rabbinic school of Gamaliel in Jerusalem (Acts 22:3), a career that rendered him so little financial security that he had to augment his livelihood by making tents (Acts 18:3). As a personal disciple at the feet of Gamaliel, Paul was under the tutelage of a scholar who is recognized even today as one of the ten greatest rabbis in Jewish history.

Next, we see that Paul was very bothered by what he considered heresy; that is why he was zealously persecuting the church. (Acts 9:2) He was adamant that the Christian movement, which he considered to be a blasphemous perversion of the Jewish faith, be crushed to death before it had a chance to spread its infectious heresy any further. He even had a role in the first martyrdom in the history of the Christian faith. (Acts 22:20)

Third, it is abundantly clear that he had the ability to teach and expound doctrine. His eloquence and clarity in expressing even the most complex concepts are evidenced through the record of his sermons and speeches in the book of Acts and in the written legacy left to us in his epistles. I find it interesting that he never quoted from his mentor Gamaliel and that he rarely made allusions to any of the other scholars he would have studied, suggesting that he had such a thorough personal grasp of the material that he didn't need to quote from other teachers' insights. Apparently, what had happened in his life was that all the formal training he had received had served more to bring the kingdom of God inside him to the surface rather than to merely teach him what others thought to be the truth.

A fourth indicator that suggests that the kingdom of God may have already been latent inside Paul is that he had relatives who were in the faith before him. In Romans 16:7, he mentioned his kinsmen Andonicus and Junia who were notable among the apostles. In verse eleven, he also mentioned another relative, Herodion. Although we know nothing more about Andonicus, Junia, and Herodion or Paul's relationship with them, it doesn't take much imagination to assume that the ever-inquisitive mind of this brilliant scholar had tried to process what he was hearing about, possibly directly from these relatives.

The fifth indicator that I see suggesting that Paul was a person of peace with the kingdom of God already inside him is found in the story of his conversion. When he encountered Jesus on the road to Damascus, he immediately called Him, *Lord*. (Acts 9:5, 9:6, 26:15) Before Jesus even identified Himself to Saul, something inside the persecutor erupted with the proclamation that he was in the presence of the Lord. As soon as Jesus introduced Himself, Saul was faced with a dilemma: his spirit recognized that Jesus was the Lord; yet, all his religious training and theology told him that Jesus was the biggest heretic to have ever appeared on the Israeli landscape. Paul immediately accepted what his spirit man told him because the kingdom of God was already active inside him, even though every indication in his external experience blatantly opposed it. Paul's next step was to go into isolation in Arabia to seek reconciliation between his spiritual revelation and his traditional theological training. Because he knew that the Old Testament was truly God's infallible Word, Paul had to find a way to reconcile what was in the scripture with what he knew to be true about Jesus. He had to unravel the scriptures from all the interpretations in which they had been entangled – interpretations that, until now, he felt to be true and accurate. Apparently, Paul knew that he needed to make this spiritual journey on his own, unguided by others' biases. Therefore, he resisted the apparently logical option of seeking counsel from the recognized leaders in the church. (Galatians 1:17) Paul returned from Arabia with a personal revelation of his own, not a parroted repertoire of others' teachings. In the isolation of the desert, he had gone through a discovery process that led him to an inalterable conviction of the doctrines he was to live by and minister to others.

Paul became a son of peace when the kingdom of God that had been bottled up inside him found its full expression and meaning in the simple revelation, "Jesus is Lord." Until he came to that revelation, the same force that later became his impetus to spread the gospel around the world was only a misdirected frustration looking for meaningful expression. Until that force inside of Paul found its true meaning, it drove Paul to extremes in the opposite direction. The same is often the case in modern-day sons and daughters of peace. Until they find meaning in their lives, they may be criminals, social activists, religious radicals, political extremists, or opinionated fanatics.

The Bible gives a few hints as to how we are to recognize sons and daughters of peace when we encounter them. Jesus recognized Nathanael as a son of peace as soon as He saw him under a fig tree. (John 1:47-50) The significance of this illustration is that the Jewish rabbis made a practice of sending their students to do their recitations under a fig tree. Apparently, Nathanael was studying the scripture when Jesus first noticed him.   The fact that Nicodemus risked his reputation as a leader in the established religion of the day by coming to see Jesus secretly at night proved that he was sincerely seeking the kingdom of God – proof that he was a true son of peace. (John 3:1-2) When Jesus came upon the woman at the well (John 4:4-26), He identified her as a daughter of peace who would immediately spread the message to all the men of Samaria (verses 27-42). The very fact that this woman continued to bounce from man to man even though it had cost her her reputation and acceptability in the city proved that she was desperate for love and would not stop looking no matter how much her quest would cost her. Jesus understood that it was more than just physical love she needed; she was on a quest for divine love because the kingdom of God was already trying to invade her heart. In Luke 9:57-62, we read the story of three individuals who volunteered to join the disciples but were not accepted because they were not sons of peace. In each case, Jesus could see that they had other kingdoms established in their hearts. Whether it was money, family, or any other earthly pursuit, their self-absorbed motivations disqualified these men from being sons of peace and, therefore, candidates for discipleship. Certainly, it was because Jesus only focused His discipleship efforts on those individuals who truly displayed the qualities of sons of peace that He was able to say at the end of His ministry that all except one of them were faithfully preserved in the faith. (John 17:12) When the multitude turned away from Jesus because they felt that His teachings were too difficult, the true disciples stayed because they realized that no one else had the words of life, a solid indicator that they were sons of peace. (John 6:60-71)

These sons and daughters of peace may come from any walk of life. As we have already noted, there could be blue-collar workers (Aquila and Priscilla), business owners (Lydia), religious leaders (Paul), social outcasts (the woman at the well), political leaders (Publius), beauty queens (Esther), and wealthy socialites (Barnabas). We can easily add to that list IRS agents (Matthew and Zacchaeus), housewives (Mary and Martha), students (Daniel and Samuel), ranchers (David and Moses), fishermen (Peter, James, and John), and any other position in life – including yours!

Discipleship Made Easy

Once a son or daughter of peace has been identified, the next focus should be to help him or her develop an experiential understanding of the gospel message. Jesus' pattern was to basically teach through stories, illustrations, and parables. The value of such teaching is captured in a modern educational model:

If you tell me, I'll forget.
If you show me, I'll remember.
If you involve me, I'll understand.

Jesus involved His disciples by telling them stories that they had to interpret, rather than simply laying out the whole message in outline format before them. Certainly, there were times such as the Sermon on the Mount when He used didactic teaching in which He conveyed specific information. He even told the disciples, when He gave full definition to the Great Commission, that they should do the same, *Teaching them to observe all things whatsoever I have commanded you.* (Matthew 28:20) He even used the Greek word *didasko*, from which we get the term "didactic," to describe how they were to communicate truth in this discipleship process. However, the bulk of His ministry was based on parables. Even Paul, who weighs in heavily as a didactic teacher, peppered his instructions with illustrations and analogies.

Mark 4:34 explains that Jesus did take the disciples aside to explain to them the full meaning of the parables, and Luke 8:9 reveals that His disciples felt comfortable asking Him for insights into the meaning of the parables. However, in John 16:29, we see how it actually startled the disciples when He spoke to them directly rather than through a story that required them to think through the meaning, *His disciples said unto him, Lo, now speakest thou plainly, and speakest no proverb.*

Going back to Matthew chapter thirteen, let's see the explanation as to why Jesus used the parabolic teaching method and find out what it produced in the disciples.

All these things spake Jesus unto the multitude in parables; and without a parable spake he not unto them: That it might be fulfilled which was spoken by the prophet, saying, I will open my mouth in parables; I will utter things which have been kept secret from the foundation of the world. (verses 34-35)
Jesus saith unto them, Have ye understood all these things? They say unto him, Yea, Lord. Then said he unto them, Therefore every scribe which is instructed unto the kingdom of heaven is like unto a man that is an householder, which bringeth forth out of his treasure things new and old. (verses 51-52)

The parables were Jesus' way of expressing eternal truths that are secrets or mysteries to the unregenerate but revelation to those who, as other scriptures would describe, have ears to hear what the Spirit is saying to the churches. (Matthew 11:15, 13:9, 13:43; Mark 4:9, 4:23, 7:16, 8:18; Luke 8:8, 14:35; Revelation 2:7, 2:11, 2:17, 2:29, 3:6, 3:13, 3:22, 13:9) On the other hand, those who do hear and are fully taken through the discipleship process are able to not only repeat what the teacher explained to them but to also expound on their own revelations from the stories. At this point, it is probably important to add that the full disciple-making process will definitely involve more than just parables and stories. Even though statistics suggest that as much as seventy percent of the Bible is made up of narratives and stories, we can't ignore the fact that the remaining thirty percent is direct didactic teaching. The prophet Isaiah insisted that teaching had to involve the line-upon-line, precept-upon-precept approach (verses 28:10-13). Aquila and Priscilla took time to instruct Apollos in the principles of the faith (Acts 18:24-28), and Paul spent two full years conducting a Bible school in Ephesus (Acts 19:9-10).

It will be those sons and daughters of peace who have

been thoroughly discipled who can then become the harvest laborers who will bring in the harvest in their nations. To illustrate the point, let's compare the results of powerful mass evangelism and the discipleship pattern that Paul set forth in II Timothy 2:2 when he told his trainee to take what he had deposited into his life and transfer it to faithful men who would follow his example and impart it to others. This sort of multiplication through reproduction produces incredible results. I believe that it is also suggested in Titus 1:5 when Paul left Titus in Crete with the specific instruction to ordain elders in every city just as he (Paul) had appointed him (Titus). I also see a hint of this discipleship model in Acts 20:17 when Paul called the elders from Ephesus to meet him in Miletus. Even though he had been separated from them for many years, there was still a bond between him and them and a recognition that what he was able to pass to them would be further communicated to the rest of the *flock* in Ephesus. (verse 28)

If you could win one thousand people per year to Jesus every year for seventeen years, you would have brought seventeen thousand individuals into the kingdom of God during your lifetime of ministry. However, if you were able to win one person every six months and disciple these new converts and teach them to also win a new convert every six months, the exponential growth of your evangelism would be that of reaching more than the world's population in the same amount of time. This is the power of exponential growth. One classic example of this simple, but powerful, multiplication principle was demonstrated when the game of chess was first invented. When the creator of the game showed his invention to the ruler of the country, the king was so pleased that he gave the inventor the right to name his prize for the invention. The man requested that one grain of rice be placed on the first square of the chessboard, two grains on the second square, four on the third square, and so forth, doubling the amount each time he moved to the next square. The ruler, mathematically naive, quickly accepted the inventor's offer, even getting offended by his perceived notion that the inventor was asking for such a seemingly low price. He ordered the treasurer to count and hand over the rice to the inventor. However, when the treasurer took more than a week to calculate the amount of rice needed, the ruler asked him for a reason for his tardiness. The treasurer then gave him the results of the calculation and explained that it would be impossible to give the inventor the reward – more than eighteen quintillion grains of rice, exceeding the world's total output. The chart on the following page shows how this discipleship method will cause the Body of Christ to explode numerically. This is the same model that God used to populate the earth in the first place. The entire world's physical population came from one family; not one man having many children, but each child having his own children. Impacting nations works exactly the same way – through bringing converts to the state of maturity where they are able to reproduce themselves in the lives of others who will, in turn, perpetuate the process. Add this reproductive growth to the results gained through evangelism, and the gospel becomes an unstoppable force in the world! If you take a look at the chart, you'll notice that the growth is fairly slow for the first five years or so; then, at that point, we reach what can be described as critical mass or a tipping point at which the slow growth begins to take quantum leaps. If we use evangelism in addition to reproduction to achieve critical mass and that tipping point quickly, then the discipleship approach is in "turbo mode" from the launch. In the book of Acts, we read that three thousand were won to Christ on the Day of Pentecost and that five thousand more came when the lame man was healed at the Gate Beautiful. If these eight thousand were carefully trained so that they could take up the one-on-one discipleship ministry, the winning of the world would be "jumped-started" by a full six and a half years!

When we moved to our home in Colorado, we were having some problems with the heat in our home. No matter what I did, I simply couldn't get the thermostat to control the temperature. After repeated calls to the company who installed the unit, I finally had to resort to asking the gentleman to come and look at the control because I could never get results from following the instructions he gave me over the phone. When he arrived, he got the system working properly in just a few seconds. Embarrassed that I had asked him to come all the way up the mountain to push a couple buttons, I got him to watch me as I demonstrated what I had been doing so futilely. Instantly, he recognized my problem. There were two control buttons that I was pushing in succession but they were supposed to be pressed at the same time. Once I knew to engage both buttons at the same time, the system worked perfectly. This same principle applies to the Great Commission; as soon as we learn to implement evangelism and discipleship at the same time, we'll discover that the Commission really is doable.

Jesus gave us three indicators to know when we are truly on track toward accomplishing the discipleship process as He intended. Notice how each of these statements defined the various elements of the discipleship process as we have been able to extract it from the gospel narratives. These characteristics may not necessarily be instilled in those who come into the Body of Christ through simple evangelism.

Involvement of the disciple in the teachings and stories of Jesus:

> *Then said Jesus to those Jews which believed on him, If ye continue in my word, then are ye my disciples indeed.* (John 8:31)

Personal commitment to one another in the discipleship process:

> *By this shall all men know that ye are my disciples, if ye have love one to another.* (John 13:35)

Reproduction as a result of the discipleship process:
> *Herein is my Father glorified, that ye bear much fruit; so shall ye be my disciples.* (John 15:8)

At this point, we are all probably thinking the same

thing, "What curriculum would be the best to use in this discipleship process?" That certainly was the issue that the Every Home for Christ team that I worked with had to address. As one of the largest evangelical ministries in the world, they were seeing millions of new believers come into the kingdom each year and thousands of new discipleship groups birthed annually. The result was that they were faced with the challenge of finding an adequate and affordable curriculum to use in the myriad of languages of the people they were reaching in ever-increasing numbers. We spent quite a lot of effort studying materials from a very wide variety of sources and eventually focused our attention on one specific approach. No matter how much the committee liked the materials, we were faced with an impossible task of making the materials fit the needs at hand. The sheer magnitude of the task before us disqualified this and all other courses we examined. Our chosen curriculum consisted of material that filled eight volumes, costing about twenty-fives dollars per set to print. In addition, it took almost two years to translate it into a new language. With 6,528 languages in the world, it would take thirteen thousand years to accomplish the translation process and incalculable resources to print and distribute the necessary copies around the world. Even though we could see the definite roadblocks, we knew that there had to be a simple solution. Eventually, we realized that every one of us was carrying the answer around with us without even realizing it. Much like the secrets to David's success over Goliath, the answer was hidden in plain sight right under our noses. It was the Bible, God's original discipleship manual. The latest statistics we were able to obtain from those working with translation efforts is that the Bible will be translated into every language on earth within thirteen years – a far cry from the thirteen thousand years needed to translate our chosen discipleship curriculum!

But, now, there was another question that we had to entertain – that of how people around the world could effectively use the Bible to disciple others without a set curriculum, an organized approach, or a training program. The answer again came from the example of Jesus Himself. Since He basically taught in parables, we realized that we would also need to focus on the use of parables in teaching and discipling the new believers across the planet. Since stories are easy to remember and retell, it seemed only logical that we should make the stories of the Bible the primary focus of the discipleship process. We realized that there is no need to simply disseminate facts and figures and label that "training" or "teaching." The true meaning of discipleship is to produce fruitful Christians who then go out and multiply through reproducing in others what God has done in them. Through this, we can disciple the nations – a task that is actually doable without an elaborate educational network or curriculum.

This approach does not eliminate didactic teaching on the doctrinal sections of the scriptures; it simply moves such teaching to a second tier where those mature believers who have taken time to do more systematic study can provide more in-depth studies. Yet, it allows new believers to discover life-changing truths and principles just as I did by exploring the story of David and Goliath.

Exponential Power of Disciple-making

Beginning	1
Six months	2
One Year	4
One Year, Six Months	8
Two Years	16
Two Years, Six Months	32
Three Years	64
Three Years, Six Months	128
Four Years	256
Four Years, Six Months	512
Five Years	1,024
Five Years, Six Months	2,048
Six Years	4,096
Six Years, Six Months	8,192
Seven Years	16,384
Seven Years, Six Months	32,768
Eight Years	65,536
Eight Years, Six Months	131,072
Nine Years	262,144
Nine Years, Six Months	524,288
Ten Years	1,048,576
Ten Years, Six Months	2,097,152
Eleven Years	4,194,304
Eleven Years, Six Months	8,388,608
Twelve Years	16,777,216
Twelve Years, Six Months	33,554,432
Thirteen Years	67,108,864
Thirteen Years, Six Months	134,217,728
Fourteen Years	268,435,456
Fourteen Years, Six Months	536,870,912
Fifteen Years	1,073,741,824
Fifteen Years, Six Months	2,147,483,648
Sixteen Years	4,294,967,296
Sixteen Years, Six Months	8,589,934,592

The Power of a Story

Just as I had discovered that there were three keys in David's approach to challenging the giant and that there were three aspects to each of these keys, the committee developing the discipleship program understood that there was also a three-pronged approach to studying a story and that each of these levels of study consisted of three specific questions to be answered. Perhaps the best way to understand this approach is to go through a Bible story asking and answering each of these questions. For that purpose, I've chosen a story that most of us have misunderstood and that is actually used in many discipleship manuals to teach something that is directly opposite to what it is intended to communicate. By simply going through these nine questions and answering them honestly without the biases we have inherited from sermons and previous teachings, we can uncover exactly what Jesus was trying to communicate. Hopefully, going through this parable with an open mind and a fresh approach will help us to see that a specifically trained or well-versed Bible teacher is not necessary to help new believers develop a strong and maturing Christian faith. The story I have chosen is Jesus' parable about prayer.

And he spake a parable unto them to this end, that men ought always to pray, and not to faint; Saying, There was in a city a judge, which feared not God, neither regarded man: And there was a widow in that city; and she came unto him, saying, Avenge me of mine adversary. And he would not for a while: but afterward he said within himself, Though I fear not God, nor regard man; Yet because this widow troubleth me, I will avenge her, lest by her continual coming she weary me. And the Lord said, Hear what the unjust judge saith. And shall not God avenge his own elect, which cry day and night unto him, though he bear long with them? I tell you that he will avenge them speedily. Nevertheless when the Son of man cometh, shall he find faith on the earth? (Luke 18:1-8)

Since this passage begins with a statement that contrasts praying against fainting and ends with the question about faith being found in the world, most teachers make what seems to be a logical deduction that the story of the widow's request of the judge is intended to teach us about diligence in prayer. The result is that almost one hundred percent of the sermons and teachings based on this text emphasize a relentless – even demanding – attitude toward prayer. This passage is used to teach us that we must become adamant and resolute with God if we don't get what we want on our first request. Teachers and preachers use this passage in such a way that it eventually suggests that an individual's ability to determinately stand his ground in prayer will eventually get him an answer. However, as inspiring as such teaching might be, this is not at all what Jesus was saying. In fact, the underlying message conveyed in such an interpretation of this story undermines our basic relationship with our heavenly Father and teaches us to rely upon our own works (prayer) rather than to have a confident faith in God. Having "upset the apple cart" with these comments, I suppose that I'd better quickly move on into looking at what the parable actually says.

The first step in analyzing a story is to know it by acquainting ourselves with exactly what the story says. To do so, we have to ask three simple questions:

Who are the characters?
What are the actions of these characters?
What are the details that give life to the story?

In the discipleship process, these and all the other questions to be addressed are answered in a casual give-and-take discussion with the one doing the discipleship, allowing the new believer to discover the answers as the teacher nudges him through the process. This present presentation requires that I give you the answers in print; however, I suggest that you take time to look through the story and come up with your own list of responses before looking at the answers I will give.

<u>Who are the characters in the story?</u>
He (Jesus)
Men
A judge
A widow
The widow's adversary
The Lord (another reference to Jesus)
God
His (God's) elect
The Son of Man (another reference to Jesus)

<u>What are the actions of the characters?</u>
He (Jesus) told the story.
Men were expected to learn to pray and not faint.
The judge refused to help the woman but eventually gave in.
The widow requested help from the judge and refused to give up until she got that help.
The Lord (Jesus) compared/contrasted the judge with God.
God avenges His elect.
The Son of Man will come, looking for faith.

<u>What are the details that give life to the story?</u>
The reason that Jesus taught the story was that men would learn to pray and not faint.
The judge had no fear of God or regard for men.
The judge himself acknowledged that he had no fear of God or regard for men.
It was because the widow's continual coming wearied him, not because of her need, that the judge eventually acted on her behalf.
Jesus called the judge unjust.
God will avenge His elect speedily.
God bears long with His elect.
The elect call upon God day and night.
The ones who call upon God are His elect, not

unrelated widows.

We've probably all heard the expression, "The devil is in the details," but the truth of the matter is that the devil actually wants to keep us out of the details because it is there that we discover the true intent of the story. By seeing the true nature of the judge, we realize that he is not intended to be a symbol of God. Therefore, the way the widow pled with him should not be seen as a symbol of the way we are to approach our heavenly Father. As we uncover the details, we begin to see that the story of the widow and the judge is actually a worst-case scenario against which we are to contrast the best-case scenario of a God who considers us His elect, rather than some wearisome stranger. Rather than neglecting our requests, He answers them speedily.

Although I've already begun to interpret the story a bit by enumerating some of the things we begin to see by looking at the details of the story, this first level of study is intended to simply acquaint us with the story itself. It is actually in the next level of the study that we are to move to understanding the story. Again, there are three questions that we must answer in this process:

What are the emotions that the characters exhibit?
What are the choices that they made or could have made?
What are the motives behind the actions and choices of the characters?

In some stories, these questions are actually answered in the text; however, in most stories, we will have to use our imaginations and try to put ourselves into the shoes of the characters, feeling the story as insiders rather than as external observers. Since each person will feel and experience the story differently, there is not a list of correct answers to these questions and caution must be taken in order that we don't go too far afield by letting our imagination run too wild. However, if we practice reasonable constraint, we should come to some logical conclusions as to the emotions, motives, and choices implied in the story.

<u>What are the emotions that the characters exhibit?</u>

The widow could have run through a gamut of emotions from desperation to fear to disappointment to anger; however, the one emotion that dominates the story is her feeling of determination and self-reliance.

The emotion of the judge is obviously frustration.

The emotion of God must be one of compassion as He views the needs of his elect.

The Son of Man may possibly experience disappointment if He does not find the faith that He is looking for in the earth. On the other hand, He may experience delight if He finds what He is looking for.

<u>What are the choices that they made or could have made?</u>

The widow obviously had the choice to give up or to continue persistently begging the judge for help.

The judge's clear options were to help the widow or to decline her plea.

God also has choices. He can act like the unjust judge and make His elect grovel while He delays in assisting them or He can immediately spring into action to answer their petitions.

<u>What are the motives behind the characters' actions and choices?</u>

The widow's motive is apparent. She has a desperate need and wants to get it answered.

The judge's motive is obviously selfishness. It is possible that he delayed his answer hoping that the widow would resort to offering him a bribe. At any rate, it was his own discomfort, not the widow's need, that finally moved him to action.

God's motivation is evidently love in that He answers the requests of His elect – those who have a relationship with Him, not some random widow who has shown up at His doorstep.

At this point, we are inside the story enough that we are actually able to understand what it is intended to communicate. The lesson we see is that we should always feel confident to pray to God. Unlike the unjust judge, God has a character of compassion and is interested in all our needs. Unlike the unrelated widow, we are His elect; therefore, He is ready and willing to answer our requests speedily. It doesn't matter when we call upon Him – during daytime business hours or even in the middle of the night – He is ready to help. If we had to rely upon our own strength to "arm wrestle" God into answering our prayers as the widow did with the unconcerned judge, we might faint in the process. Because we often do take this self-reliant attitude toward Him, God does have to bear long with us, hoping that we will eventually catch on to the generous relationship He so graciously extends to us. The Son of Man is looking for faith, a confident trust in God. But will He find that in the earth, or will He find the earth populated with people whose confidence is in their own stamina and ability to persistently argue their case before a God with whom they have no true or intimate relationship?

Now that we know the story and have begun to understand it, we still have one more level that we must explore before we have completed the discipleship process. We must apply the story. Here, again, there are three questions that must be addressed in the process. These questions come from the words of the Apostle Paul in II Timothy 3:16-17.

All scripture is given by inspiration of God, and is profitable for doctrine, for reproof, for correction, for instruction in righteousness: That the man of God may be perfect, throughly furnished unto all good works.

It sounds as if the apostle had disciple-making in the forefront of his mind as he wrote about scripture as being profitable for the ultimate purpose of producing men and women who are perfect and thoroughly furnished for all good works – a perfect description of those who have successfully gone through the discipleship process. The three questions we use to apply the scripture to our lives answer the specific aspects for which Paul says scripture is profitable. He first mentions doctrine or teaching, as other translations render his wording. This is the overall educational process covered through all three stages of the exploration process; however, the remaining three aspects are specific to this last stage of application. Reproof, which has to do with our past actions, challenges us to look back to see what we have done wrong in the past. Correction has to do with the present, asking us to discover how we can remedy our past errors. Instruction in righteousness relates to the future as we develop a plan for moving forward, free from these faults and enabled not to repeat them. Our three questions for applying the truths of the story to our lives are:

> What have I done wrong in the past?
> How can I correct these errors today?
> How can I ensure that I don't repeat these errors in the future?

Obviously, the answers to these questions will vary with each individual student; however, allow me to list the answers as I would personally respond because I believe that my answers might not be too far afield from those of anyone who has taken an unbiased look at the story and has honestly let it speak to him.

What have I done wrong in the past?
> I have erroneously interpreted the story to imply that I need to beg God to answer my prayers and that it is really my persistence in prayer (works) rather than God's love (grace) that gets results.

How can I correct these errors today?
> I must change my mental perception of God in order to know how to effectively approach Him with true faith when I pray.

How can I ensure that I don't repeat these errors in the

future?

Since I know that the only true source of information that can change my way of thinking and life is the Bible, I must find scriptures to use as anchor points for renewing my mind so that I don't fall back into my natural, carnal point of view. I will memorize them and apply them when making requests of the Lord. Second Chronicles 16:9, *For the eyes of the LORD run to and fro throughout the whole earth, to shew himself strong in the behalf of them whose heart is perfect toward him*, tells me that God (unlike the unjust judge who didn't want to be bothered by the widow's problem) is actually looking for a chance to get involved in helping me. John 3:16, *For God so loved the world, that he gave his only begotten Son, that whosoever believeth in him should not perish, but have everlasting life*, tells me that, because of His extreme love for me, God spared no expense in rescuing me from my sins. Romans 8:32, *He that spared not his own Son, but delivered him up for us all, how shall he not with him also freely give us all things?* furthers that truth by telling me that, if He was willing to give His Son for me, He will certainly take care of anything that requires much less expense on His part. Isaiah 65:24, *It shall come to pass, that before they call, I will answer; and while they are yet speaking, I will hear*, and Matthew 6:8, *Your Father knoweth what things ye have need of, before ye ask him*, assure me that I don't have to beg, plead, or be dramatic to get God's attention; He is already attentive to my need – even before I make my requests. Secondly, I will constantly remind myself of who I am to God. I am not a widow; rather, I am His bride for whom He has given Himself. (Ephesians 5:25) If He gave Himself, certainly He will not turn a deaf or unconcerned ear to my needs and petitions.

Who would have ever thought that we could gain so much practical instruction for living from one simple Bible story and nine little questions? And even more, we were able to do so without being highly trained Bible scholars. This is proof positive that disciple-making is no more difficult than witnessing or evangelism. It can be done without extensive preparation or a fully developed curriculum. All it takes is an unbiased mind and a heart open to the voice of the Holy Spirit.

Remember that one of the significant elements in disciple-making was the necessity of a genuine commitment between the one doing the discipleship and the new believer. If such a relationship exists to the level that the two can sit together and explore the revelations in one Bible story each day, they will have covered over one hundred eighty stories in the process of six months, the time span I suggested earlier. Imagine how far along the new believer will be in his Christian faith by the time he has dug out the truths in that many scriptures and put a plan in place to ensure that he is constantly applying them to his life. Certainly, he'll be well on his way to perfection and fairly well furnished for all good works by that point. Without a doubt, he'll be ready to find at least one more person with whom he can share the joy and adventure of exploring the scriptures and discovering their truths. The next grain of rice will be added to the chessboard, and we'll be one step closer to conquering the giant challenges of discipling the nations and accomplishing the Great Commission.

The passage in II Timothy that I quoted in the section about the application questions states that all scripture is profitable for doctrine, for reproof, for correction, for instruction in righteousness; therefore, it would be totally appropriate to simply hand a Bible to the new convert and the individual who is discipling him and let them pick Bible stories at random to study. However, it seems a bit more logical to guide them through certain significant topics in the initial stages of their discovery process. Therefore, we spent some considerable time and effort perusing other discipleship courses and doctrinal statements (such as the Apostles' Creed, the Westminster Confession, and the statements of faith of all the major Christian denominations) in a quest to find what topics seemed to be most commonly recognized as the essentials of the Christian faith. The result of that study was a fifty-two-lesson study divided into four parts. The four divisions were modeled after the pattern of a house, based on Paul's illustration in Ephesians 2:20 where he says that our faith is a structure built upon the doctrines of the apostles. The first thirteen lessons are the cornerstone that is the identifying mark of the Christian faith – those teachings that set our faith apart from other world religions and philosophies. The second set of thirteen lessons constitutes the foundation – those truths upon which all else rests. The thirteen lessons in the walls section are those elements that outsiders observe as they see Christians living their daily lives. The final thirteen lessons in this portion of the study make up the roof – scriptural truths that prevent the entrance of false doctrine just as a roof serves as a protective shield over a home to keep out the destructive elements. After these four essential segments are covered, all following lessons are considered as interior topics – studies that can be selected according to the specific needs and interests of the individuals, just as the owners of a home can make their own decisions about how to arrange and decorate the interior of their personal homes.

One aspect that the development team was very sensitive to was the fact that much of the scripture is not in story form and that such didactic teaching must be incorporated in order to have a thorough understanding of the gospel. Therefore, each lesson is accompanied with a list of additional scriptures on the topic so that the instructor and student can make a more thorough study of the topic and, therefore, obtain a more well-rounded view of what the scriptures have to say about each truth. To learn more about the Be Fruitful and Multiply approach, please google "every home discovery method."

Appendix I contains in skeletal form – title, scriptural reference for the story (in bold print), and additional scripture references (in normal print) – the fifty-two lessons in the original Be Fruitful and Multiply series, along with an additional one hundred thirty-one lessons, constituting enough lessons to carry a new believer through one story each day for the six months suggested in the discipleship model presented earlier in this book. The additional lessons I have added take the new convert through several interior category studies [lessons 53-71], a study of the life of the early church as depicted in the book of Acts as a pattern for the present-day church [lessons 72-84], a series on the fruit of the Spirit [lessons 85-93], an analysis of the commandments of Jesus (since Jesus specifically listed this as part of the discipleship process in Matthew 28:20) [lessons 94-141], and the parables of Jesus [lessons 142-183].

I pray that, when you come to the end of the prose section of this volume, you don't assume that you have finished the book. In all actuality, everything else in this book is little more than introductory material to prepare you for the next step. Please go to the appendix, pick a lesson or two at random and take a few minutes – or a few hours – to explore the truths in the story by applying the nine questions to the passage. Take the time to carefully examine each detail and to investigate every possible motive, emotion, and choice in the story. Be sure to look up the additional study scriptures and even add your own additional scriptures by using your concordance to follow up the key words, thoughts, and ideas in the story. If your Bible has cross-references, invest the time and effort to look them up. I'm certain that you'll find the study so rewarding that you'll find yourself wanting to go through the other hundred eighty stories and then plunge into the other stories you'll find on your own in the Bible. But please don't stop there. Ask the Lord to show you the sons and daughters of peace around you who already have a heart's desire to find the kingdom of God. Invite them to join you in your journey through the scripture and, in doing so, you'll bring the Body of Christ one step closer to fulfilling Jesus' Great Commission and discipling your nation.

Empowered

Just prior to His ascension, Jesus appeared to the disciples in Jerusalem and emphasized another dimension of the Great Commission – the need to be supernaturally empowered for the task before them. He then led them to the Mount of Olives where He reemphasized this same aspect one last time before He left them. Jesus knew that in order to really be effective, we would need a special anointing from God and a passion birthed from the Holy Spirit – the fire of God upon our lives.

To understand the fire of God in our lives, a good place to begin might be with the prophet Elijah as he called that fire down on the summit of Mount Carmel.

And Elijah came unto all the people, and said, How long halt ye between two opinions? if the LORD be God, follow him: but if Baal, then follow him. And the people answered him not a word. Then said Elijah unto the people, I, even I only, remain a prophet of the LORD; but Baal's prophets are four hundred and fifty men. Let them therefore give us two bullocks; and let them choose one bullock for themselves, and cut it in pieces, and lay it on wood, and put no fire under: and I will dress the other bullock, and lay it on wood, and put no fire under: And call ye on the name of your gods, and I will call on the name of the LORD: and the God that answereth by fire, let him be God. And all the people answered and said, It is well spoken. And Elijah said unto the prophets of Baal, Choose you one bullock for yourselves, and dress it first; for ye are many; and call on the name of your gods, but put no fire under. And they took the bullock which was given them, and they dressed it, and called on the name of Baal from morning even until noon, saying, O Baal, hear us. But there was no voice, nor any that answered. And they leaped upon the altar which was made. And it came to pass at noon, that Elijah mocked them, and said, Cry aloud: for he is a god; either he is talking, or he is pursuing, or he is in a journey, or peradventure he sleepeth, and must be awaked. And they cried aloud, and cut themselves after their manner with knives and lancets, till the blood gushed out upon them. And it came to pass, when midday was past, and they prophesied until the time of the offering of the evening sacrifice, that there was neither voice, nor any to answer, nor any that regarded. And Elijah said unto all the people, Come near unto me. And all the people came near unto him. And he repaired the altar of the LORD that was broken down. And Elijah took twelve stones, according to the number of the tribes of the sons of Jacob, unto whom the word of the LORD came, saying, Israel shall be thy name: And with the stones he built an altar in the name of the LORD: and he made a trench about the altar, as great as would contain two measures of seed. And he put the wood in order, and cut the bullock in pieces, and laid him on the wood, and said, Fill four barrels with water, and pour it on the burnt sacrifice, and on the wood. And he said, Do it the second time. And they did it the second time. And he said, Do it the third time. And they did it the third time. And the water ran round about the altar; and he filled the trench also with water. And it came to pass at the time of the offering of the evening sacrifice, that Elijah the prophet came near, and said, LORD God of Abraham, Isaac, and of Israel, let it be known this day that thou art God in Israel, and that I am thy servant, and that I have done all these things at thy word. Hear me, O LORD, hear me, that this people may know that thou art the LORD God, and that thou hast turned their heart back again. Then the fire of the LORD fell, and consumed the burnt sacrifice, and the wood, and the stones, and the dust, and licked up the water that was in the trench.

And when all the people saw it, they fell on their faces: and they said, The LORD, he is the God; the LORD, he is the God. (I Kings 18:21-39)

The story of Elijah's encounter with the prophets of Baal is one of remarkable courage and confidence in God. The prophet single-handedly and courageously took on over four hundred pagan priests. His challenge to them was simple and straightforward: call down fire from heaven. "Simple?" you may ask. Yes, simple – well, at least for the prophet who understood the nature of God. You see, for some, it is easy to believe in and expect healing because they understand the nature of God as Jehovah Rapha, the God who heals. For others, believing for financial provision is "no sweat" because they understand the nature of God as Jehovah Jirah, the God who provides. In Elijah's case, he must have had a revelation that his God is a consuming fire. (Deuteronomy 4:24, 9:3) Surely, the prophet was aware that God had chosen to reveal Himself through fire since the first few pages of the Bible tell of when He appeared as a pillar of fire each night as He led the Israelites out of Egyptian bondage. (Exodus 13:21-22, 14:24; Numbers 14:14) Certainly, the prophet would not have been surprised to see the same trend recurring if he had also been able to read the New Testament in which God chooses to manifest Himself in fire right up to the very last few pages. (Revelation 19:12, 20:9) Knowing that fire is the very nature of God must have made the prophet confident that he could call upon Him and expect Him to show up as a roaring blaze to consume his sacrifice.

The interesting thing about the fire of God is that it is not some magical characteristic of a superhero that we humans observe from afar and "oooh" and "aaah" like a Fourth of July firework display. Rather, the fire of God is intended to intimately affect us and permeate every aspect of our lives and ministries. One cigarette company used to advertise its products as having flavor that penetrated over, under, around, and through the tobacco. In the same way, God's purpose is that His people would experience His fire over, under, around, and through their lives.

On the day of Pentecost, miraculous cloven tongues of fire suddenly appeared above the heads of all who were gathered in the Upper Room. (Acts 2:3) This was the fire of God over them to improve them. Just think for a moment who it was that comprised that crowd of one hundred and twenty individuals. Most notable were the eleven disciples who had, just a few days prior, fled in terror when the angry mob appeared to arrest their leader, abandoning Him to the bloodthirsty crowd and the murderous priestly court. Peter, their most ardent spokesman, had boasted that he would die before he would allow any harm to come to the Master; yet, he not only fled from the scene – he denied three times that he even knew Him and even added a few choice swear words to emphasize his statements. Not only were they cowards, deserters, and, in the case of Peter, an empty braggart and a traitor; they were also selfish sluggards who repeatedly fell asleep as their friend depended on them for moral and spiritual support as He struggled through His agonizing prayer in Gethsemane. They were fearful unbelievers who hid behind locked doors and rebuffed those who came with reports of the Lord's resurrection. But, now that they had been touched by the fire of God that hovered over them, they were improved! Suddenly, they were supercharged with a new boldness that propelled them fearlessly around the world into the most hostile situations to proclaim the message of the One whom they had so readily denied. Peter, the one who had run fastest and hardest, now stood up and publicly proclaimed to the crowd that had gathered on that Pentecost Sunday that they were the ones guilty of having killed Jesus. He unabashedly accused them of bloodguilt and demanded their repentance. (Acts 2:36-38) What a change! A transformation had taken place in him. The fire of God over him had done its work of improving him.

Malachi, the prophet who rounded out the Old Testament, addressed the issue of a fire that God can set under His people to remove any harmful and unwanted elements. In

106

verse two of chapter three, Malachi talks to us about the fire that a refiner uses to purify his metal. After placing the ore in a crucible, the refiner heats the apparatus until it is white hot, almost transparent, in the flames. As the temperature rises, many of the impurities reach the point of spontaneous combustion and burst into flames and evaporate before the refiner's eyes. Other impurities simply float to the top where the metallurgist can skim them off with his spatula. This fire of God under us is a purifying fire that is intended to remove any and all ungodly thoughts, attitudes, and actions out of our lives.

When John the Baptist pronounced the coming of Jesus as the messiah, he added that although his personal ministry was one of baptizing in water, Jesus would baptize in the Holy Ghost and fire. A rather traditional Pentecostal interpretation of the concept of the baptism in fire has been a super-duper anointing which enabled the believer to run around the church, jump the pews, and shout loudly. However, even a cursory look at the context of the passages reveals that this simply is not what John was talking about. The Baptist goes on to explain, *Whose fan is in his hand, and he will thoroughly purge his floor, and gather his wheat into the garner; but he will burn up the chaff with unquenchable fire.* (Matthew 3:12) This baptism of fire refers directly to the practice of burning the useless chaff once it has been separated from the edible grain, a purifying very similar in nature to the refiner's fire.

Isaiah experienced this cleansing fire when he first began to make excuses to avoid the call God had placed upon his life. When he argued with God that he could not speak on His behalf since he was a man of unclean lips, a seraph touched his lips with a white-hot coal from the fire upon the altar of God. The result was instantaneous. Immediately, the prophet responded, *Here am I; send me*, the result of a purifying touch from the fire of God. (Isaiah 6:8)

The tobacco commercial goes on to speak of "around." Likewise, the Lord is a fire that is around His people to prove that they are actually His people.

By the time he had spent forty years tending sheep in the desert, Moses had likely lost all sense of self-worth. Having once stood at that lonely place at the top of the socio-economic pyramid as a member of the royal family of the most powerful nation on the face of Planet Earth, he undoubtedly walked, talked, and carried himself with an air of importance and significance. But, by now, any sense of importance was simply a dusty memory. But, then, something unusual happened to this desert shepherd; he noticed a burning bush. Unlike anything he had ever seen before – this bush continued to crackle as the flames leapt from each branch and twig, but nothing seemed to be consumed by the blaze. As he stepped forward to examine this anomaly, Moses suddenly realized that – like Alice and her magical looking glass and the children in the Chronicles of Narnia and their mysterious wardrobe – he had suddenly stepped through a dimension-wall into a new reality. This fire which consumes yet doesn't destroy is a God quality that identifies His own and sets them apart from others as a whole new breed. After his encounter with this unusual fire and the God who spoke through it, Moses – for the first time in four decades – felt significant again. At long last, he felt as if he really could be the deliverer he had tried to become so many years ago. This unusual fire assured him that he was indeed God's man and gave him a new spiritual stamina that made others take note of him. Acts 4:13 records what must have been a touch of that same fire, *Now when they saw the boldness of Peter and John, and perceived that they were unlearned and ignorant men, they marvelled; and they took knowledge of them, that they had been with Jesus.*

The last preposition applied to the tobacco advertisement is "through." God also sends His fire through believers to move them. A great example of this is Jeremiah who decided that he couldn't take the heat that society was putting on him as he prophesied their impending doom. Finally, he got so discouraged that he stepped outside his office and pulled down his shingle, "Jeremiah, prophet of God." The record of his testimony reads, *Then I said, I will not make mention of him, nor speak any more in his name. But his word was in mine heart as a burning fire shut up in my bones, and I was weary with forbearing, and I could not stay.* (Jeremiah 20:9) The factor he hadn't calculated into the equation when he resigned his position as God's spokesman was the fire that was racing through his insides. Like it did in the life of the prophet, that fire of God running through us also moves us to operate in the divine unction of God to impact our world.

The fire that surges through us is the anointing and operation of the gifts of the Spirit that enable us to move in the power of God in this physical world. Unfortunately, many of us have felt that this fire should be reserved only for use within the walls of our church buildings. To the contrary, the book of Acts records that the fire flowing through the apostles burned fiercely no matter where they were. As Peter strolled down a street, people were healed just by contact with his shadow. (Acts 5:15) Paul stirred up demons by simply walking through town. (Acts 16:16-18) A rather humorous example from my own experience was the day my wife and I met a lady on an elevator in a beachfront hotel. For some reason, she mentioned that she was not having a good time on her vacation because she had been suffering from a terrible headache for three days. Peggy touched her, assuring her that Jesus was willing to heal her. About that time, the door opened and we stepped out to head for the beach. A few minutes later, we heard a shout from the fifth floor as the woman realized that her pain was totally gone! It doesn't matter if you are in your sandals and bathing suit; if the fire of God is surging through your inner man, it will move you to act on His behalf any time and any place. That fire can flare up like the saying on the old TV show <u>Candid Camera</u>, "when you least expect it."

What is probably the most startling truth that God wants us to know about His fire is that His ultimate intent is to actually transform us into that fire. According to Psalm 104:4 and Hebrews 1:7, it is His plan to make His ministers into flames of fire. He is not willing to settle for ministers who have experienced fire, but ones who are actually the fire themselves. Too long we have settled for, "Lord, send the fire," or "Lord, let me experience the fire." God is expecting us to pray, "Lord, make me a fire." God is looking for more than just what happens to us, on us, or through us; He desires that our whole lives and personalities be characterized by His fire. We cannot settle for being carriers of the fire, lest we lose it. Nor can we be satisfied to be on fire, least we burn up. We need to be transformed into the fire itself because there is no limit to what God will do in, through, and for us when we become fire.

Let's look back at the story of Elijah on Mount Carmel for a couple summation points. First, note the reaction of the people when the prophet initially challenged them to decide between Jehovah and Baal – they answered him nothing. (verse 21) In other words, they were not moved or motivated by his ministry or challenge. Next, notice how the entire congregation fell on their faces and cried out, *The Lord, he is the God. The Lord, he is the God*, when they encountered the fire. (verse 39) If we want God to be manifested in our world, it will only happen when His fire is demonstrable and demonstrated though us. At that point, we discover that the Great Commission really is doable.

Ablaze with Passion

Perhaps a more twenty-first century word for the fire of God would be "passion." The very word somehow stirs our inner emotions and arouses something inside us. It is amazing at how often we run across the term "passion" in our daily reading. It appears almost every day in various contexts concerning sports, politics, and regular news articles. Even movie reviews occasionally mention <u>The Passion of the Christ</u> as a comparison when reviewing the religiously based movies that have recently become popular. Not only is the sheer frequency of the appearances of the term notable, the number of different contexts in which the word appears and the wide variety of meanings it carries are also astounding.

Let's begin with the movie reviews and look at Mel Gibson's use of the word. In the title of his movie, "passion" is used with its old English meaning of suffering that we often see used during Lent and the Easter season in such terms as "the Passion Week" or "Passion Play." This use of the term appears once in the <u>King James Bible</u> in Acts 1:3, *To whom also he shewed himself alive after his passion by many infallible proofs, being seen of them forty days, and speaking of the things pertaining to the kingdom of God.* <u>The Bible in Basic English</u> also uses this wording in Job 6:2, *If only my passion might be measured, and put into the scales against my trouble!* The Greek word *pascho*, which is translated as "passion" in the passage in Acts, appears fifty-two other times in the New Testament and is consistently translated to speak of suffering. (See Appendix II)

A second use of the term which often comes as a surprise is the meaning as it is used in such references as "crimes of passion," denoting anger. This usage of the term appears frequently in <u>The Bible in Basic English</u>, and occasionally in other versions such as <u>Montgomery's New Testament</u>, <u>Darby's Translation</u>, and <u>Weymouth's New</u>

Testament. (See Appendix III)

Another use of the word that might seem a bit unusual is its connotation of human qualities as opposed to any divine or supernatural character. Based on the Greek word *homoiopathes*, literally meaning "with the emotions of a human," this term appears once in the King James Version of the New Testament, *And saying, Sirs, why do ye these things? We also are men of like passions with you, and preach unto you that ye should turn from these vanities unto the living God, which made heaven, and earth, and the sea, and all things that are therein,* (Acts 14:15) and once in the Modern King James Version, *Elijah was a man of like passion as we are. And he prayed earnestly that it might not rain, and it did not rain on the earth for the time of three years and six months.* (James 5:17)

The term also denotes emotion, frequently in a negative light. While the King James Version renders the term in Mark 14:31 *more vehemently,* The Bible in Basic English translates the passage, *But he said with passion, If I have to be put to death with you, I will not be false to you. And they all said the same.* At least a dozen times each, the term is interpreted to mean either jealousy or envy. (See Appendix IV)

Probably the most common idea conveyed by the word "passion" is the thought of sexual desire and lust. Though the King James Bible does not use the term when translating these passages, such versions as the Twentieth Century New Testament, Montgomery's New Testament, the Revised Standard Version, Weymouth's New Testament, The Bible in Basic English, Darby's Translation, the American Standard Version, and Young's Literal Translation use "passion" in an abundance of such passages. But let's leave that discussion for another context and focus on the passion God places inside us for His work. The Bible in Basic English uses "passion" in a number of verses to communicate the concept of zeal or driving motivation.

Through Phinehas, and because of his passion for my honour, my wrath has been turned away from the children of Israel, so that I have not sent destruction on them all in my wrath. (Numbers 25:11)

Then the king sent for the Gibeonites; (now the Gibeonites were not of the children of Israel, but were the last of the Amorites, to whom the children of Israel had given an oath; but Saul, in his passion for the children of Israel and Judah, had made an attempt on their lives:) (II Samuel 21:2)

I am on fire with passion for your house (For the zeal of thine house hath eaten me up – KJV); and the hard things which are said about you have come on me. (Psalm 69:9)

The passion of my soul's desire is for the house of the Lord (My soul longeth, yea, even fainteth for the courts of the LORD – KJV); my heart and my flesh are crying out for the living God. (Psalm 84:2)

And it came to the minds of the disciples that the writings say, I am on fire with passion for your house. (John 2:17)

Notice the wording of Psalm 69:9 and its New Testament counterpart in John 2:17: *I am on fire with passion.* The idea of being set ablaze with passion is reminiscent of Jeremiah's summation of how the Word of God was the driving force in his life. (verse 20:9) A similar thought is suggested in the story of the two men who walked with the Risen Lord on the road to Emmaus when they summed up their encounter with Him, *Did not our heart burn within us, while he talked with us by the way, and while he opened to us the scriptures?* (Luke 24:32) John Wesley echoed their testimony when he chronicled a journal entry concerning his conversion to Christ on May 24, 1783:

In the evening, I went very unwillingly to a society in Aldersgate Street, where one was reading Luther's preface to the Epistle to the Romans. About a quarter before nine, while he was describing the change which God works in the heart through faith in Christ, I felt my heart strangely warmed. I felt I did trust in Christ, Christ alone for salvation, and an assurance was given me that he had taken away my sins, even mine, and saved me from the law of sin and death.

In each of these cases, something kindled a fervent motivation for a cause or purpose in their hearts. The question is, "How does this happen and what is it that can set a person's heart ablaze with such a passion for his cause?" If we can find any consistent point in each of these examples, it would be the Word of God. For Jeremiah, it was the internalized Word; for the disciples on the road, it was the preached Word; for Wesley, it was the written Word. Certainly, Phinehas, King Saul, and the Psalmist also shared this one common factor of the Word of God as a kindling force for passion in their lives. Phinehas, as the grandson of the high priest Aaron and the great nephew of the lawgiver Moses, had been raised in an environment saturated with the Word of God. Saul, as the king of Israel, had handwritten a personal copy of the Torah as his own personal guidebook for life. (Deuteronomy 17:18) David had not only studied the Word for his own correction and instruction (Psalm 119:11), he also authored a major portion of the book of Psalms. Just as passion in marriage is kindled by our words to each other, it is God's Word to His church that ignites passion in our lives. Just as the way we talk to our mates determines the passion in our relationship, it is the Word that we allow the Lord to speak into our hearts that determines the passion we will have in our relationship with Him.

Some two millennia ago, the Apostle John was serving time on the penal island of Patmos when the Risen Lord visited him and gave him messages for the seven churches in Turkey that he served as overseer.

Many Bible scholars have analyzed the messages given to the seven churches in chapters two and three as a prediction of the history of the church. They see the church at Ephesus (chapter 2:1-7) as depicting the zealous newly birthed church during its first century and a half (AD 30 to AD 170). The Smyrna church (chapter 2:8-11) is seen as representing the period of great persecution under the iron fist of Rome (AD 170 through AD 312). The compromising church of Pergamos (chapter 2:12-17) is designated as a representative of the period when Christianity became the official religion of the Roman Empire and, therefore, made many concessions to the secular government (AD 312 to approximately AD 600). Thyatira (chapter 2:18-29), at least to the Protestant authors, represents the thousand years that the Roman Catholic Church – in their mind, the harlot church – dominated the scene (AD 600 until 1517). The church at Sardis (chapter 3:1-6) is spoken of as being dead even though it was seen as alive and as needing to strengthen the things that were ready to die. To the scholars who have characterized these churches as depicting various stages in church history, this church stands for the Reformation period when the church was struggling to come back to life (AD 1517 through AD 1750). The Philadelphia church (chapter 3:7-13) which had an open door set before it is seen as representing the period of great mission expansion beginning with William Carey and continuing through the twentieth century (AD 1750 through AD 2000). The last church in the sequence is the lukewarm Laodicean church (chapter 3:14-22) that Jesus sees as so detestable that He vomits it up. Unfortunately, the only period of history left to relegate to this church is our present generation.

In each of these letters, the Lord addressed issues that are not unique to the churches distanced from us by two millennia nor characteristic to only certain periods of history. The real truth is that He exposed conditions that have existed throughout the history of the Christian church and continue in congregations today. Those words of correction and encouragement are just as vital for us today as they were when the ink was still wet on the apostle's parchment. In fact, that is why He ended each letter with the admonition that those who have ears to hear must hear what the Holy Spirit is saying to the churches. Notice that He did not instruct us to hear what the Spirit is saying to any individual church depicting our specific pigeonhole in history; rather, He directed us to hear what He is saying to all the churches.

It is no coincidence that each of these messages ended with the command that those who have ears should hear what the Spirit is saying to the churches. It was the power of the Word of God that was to affect each church and bring about the desired spiritual result. Interestingly enough, if we look carefully at the message to each church, we can discover that each letter centers around one of the meanings of the word "passion." I believe that we can make our own decision as to which letter best fits our individual lives by choosing which definition of "passion" to focus on. Personally, I choose the Philadelphian church as my role model. And I believe that that choice will help me to actually achieve my goal of accomplishing the Great Commission.

The letter to the church at Smyrna speaks of the passion of suffering when it describes the church as enduring tribulation, being tried, and being cast into prison. (Revelation 2:8-11) Passionate anger is expressed in the letter to the congregation at Pergamos when God Himself expresses His hatred against the doctrine of Balaam and of the Nicolaitans and when He threatens to come personally and fight against them. (Revelation 2:12-17) Passion, as human nature as opposed to divine nature, is revealed in the letter to the church at Laodicea where the congregation was so human or carnally minded that they could not even perceive of themselves as God saw them. Their human evaluation of themselves was that they were rich, increased with goods, and in need of nothing. Unfortunately, the truth was that they were actually wretched, miserable, poor, blind, and naked. They were so caught up in their human emotions that they had actually locked Jesus out of their lives. (Revelation 3:14-22) When Jesus addressed the church at Sardis, He found that they had works but that these works were not perfect before God. Even though they had passion in that they were working for the Lord, it seems that this passion must have originated from hearts that were less than perfect. Perhaps theirs was the negative passion of

116

jealousy and envy. (Revelation 3:1-6) The letter to the church at Thyatira goes even one step further in addressing the negative nature of passion when the spotlight is focused on the issue of the perverted passion of lust. In this letter, the Risen Lord exposes the problem of a self-proclaimed prophetess who seduced the people into committing fornication and adultery. (Revelation 2:18-29)

The favorable nature of passion as a driving force for a cause is discussed in the two remaining churches. Although both these churches had the positive kind of passion, one had it in a positive way while the other possessed it in a negative way. The church at Ephesus had a misdirected passion in that they loved the work of the Lord but not the Lord of the work. It seems that they had invested so much of their time and energy in fighting heresy and exposing hypocrisy within the ministry that they had let the most important fire of all dwindle – they had left their first love, their passion for Christ Himself! (Revelation 2:1-7)

Our one remaining church, the one in Philadelphia, demonstrates passion as God would desire it to operate in the lives of His people. (Revelation 3:7-13) The first thing that we notice about this church is that the Lord has nothing negative to say about it. It is only this church and the persecuted church in Smyrna who escape accusation and correction in their addresses from Jesus. The second notable characteristic about the letter to this church is the open door that Jesus has set before them. But, before we discuss this door, it is necessary that we consider the key that Jesus had used to unlock it. This key is called the *key of David*, an apparent reference to Isaiah 22:22, *And the key of the house of David will I lay upon his shoulder; so he shall open, and none shall shut; and he shall shut, and none shall open.* In this verse, the prophet is making reference to Eliakim, the son of Hilkiah, as the one who was to receive this supernatural key. This biblical character's historic role is recounted twice: in II Kings chapters eighteen and nineteen and again in Isaiah chapters thirty-six and thirty-seven. His significant contribution was the stance he took against the Assyrian messenger who tried to intimidate the people of Jerusalem into surrendering to his army. Eliakim stood up to him with faith and confidence in God until the Lord caused the invading army to miraculously retreat. Though the scriptures do not specifically identify what this key was, it is easy for us to look back into the life of David and find one characteristic that seems to stand out in his life that could have made the difference between him and any others who lacked this quality. It is likely that we need not go any further than the criteria set for his selection for the throne of Israel. After Samuel had surveyed the seven older sons of Jesse without finding a worthy candidate, the Lord revealed to him that he was looking at the wrong score card when evaluating his options. God made His point that the heart of the matter is actually the matter of the heart.

> *But the LORD said unto Samuel, Look not on his countenance, or on the height of his stature; because I have refused him: for the LORD seeth not as man seeth; for man looketh on the outward appearance, but the LORD looketh on the heart.* (I Samuel 16:7)

David obviously understood that this was his key to success and determined to keep his heart in a perfect relationship with His God. *I will behave myself wisely in a perfect way. O when wilt thou come unto me? I will walk within my house with a perfect heart.* (Psalm 101:2) Even after he sinned with Bathsheba and had her husband killed, the king's prayer was that God would re-establish his heart before Him. (Psalm 51:10) Consequently, the New Testament characterizes David as being a man after God's own heart. (Acts 13:22) He also desired to pass this spiritual key on to his son Solomon who was to succeed him on the throne. First Chronicles 28:9 records David's instructions to Solomon that he serve the Lord with a perfect heart. In verse nineteen of the following chapter, we find David in prayer for his son, interceding that the Lord would give him a perfect heart. Unfortunately, the biblical summation of Solomon's life is that *his heart was not perfect with the LORD his God, as was the heart of David his father.* (I Kings 11:4)

In the testimony of one of the subsequent kings, we get a glimpse of the problem that also plagued the Ephesian church – misdirected passion. Second Chronicles 25:2 records that Amaziah did that which was right in the sight of the Lord, yet not with a perfect heart. Like the saints at Ephesus, he was passionate in his campaign to stamp out idolatry, yet he failed to passionately pursue the Lord Himself. Because of this, he – like Asa before him – failed to obtain what is likely the greatest promise in the scripture: *The eyes of the LORD run to and fro throughout the whole earth, to shew himself strong in the behalf of them whose heart is perfect toward him.* (II Chronicles 16:9) This is the universal blessing and promise of intervention by God that can only be unlocked with the key of David – a perfect heart before the Lord – and was the promise extended to the church at Philadelphia.

One other unique quality that we notice about the church at Philadelphia is that, of all seven churches, it is the only one indicated as having any relationship to the Word of God. Not only that, they are twice commended for their faithfulness to God's Word. (verses 3:8 and 3:10) It is obviously more than a coincidence that the one significant trait we observed when we studied the passionate zeal of Phinehas, Saul, David, Jeremiah, the disciples on the road to Emmaus, and John Wesley was the Word of God! Though all seven churches are admonished to hear what the Spirit is saying, apparently only this one listened and heeded. Like David, they recognized that the key to having a perfect heart was to hide God's Word in their hearts. (Psalm 119:11) For them – and for us – the key to the kingdom is a passionate love for the Word of God and the God of the Word.

The Philadelphia church had an open door to the world set before them because of the passion that burned inside them. We, too, will find that no door can be shut if we are really passionate about the Great Commission – but, more importantly, for the One who gave it to us. (I Corinthians 16:9,

119

II Corinthians 2:12, Colossians 4:3) Passion will make the Commission doable!

Conclusion

A number of passages in the New Testament indicate that the believers in that generation did a pretty good job of spreading the message through all the nations of their day:

And there were dwelling at Jerusalem Jews, devout men, out of every nation under heaven. (Acts 2:5)

First, I thank my God through Jesus Christ for you all, that your faith is spoken of throughout the whole world. (Romans 1:8)

Through mighty signs and wonders, by the power of the Spirit of God; so that from Jerusalem, and round about unto Illyricum, I have fully preached the gospel of Christ. Yea, so have I strived to preach the gospel, not where Christ was named, lest I should build upon another man's foundation: But as it is written, To whom he was not spoken of, they shall see: and they that have not heard shall understand. For which cause also I have been much hindered from coming to you. But now having no more place in these parts, and having a great desire these many years to come unto you. (Romans 15:19-23)

If ye continue in the faith grounded and settled, and be not moved away from the hope of the gospel, which ye have heard, and which was preached to every creature which is under heaven; whereof I Paul am made a minister. (Colossians 1:23)

For from you sounded out the word of the Lord not only in Macedonia and Achaia, but also in every place your faith to God-ward is spread abroad; so that we need not to speak any thing. (I Thessalonians 1:8)

Jesus also told us that there would be another generation who would accomplish the same universal challenge in their day:

And this gospel of the kingdom shall be preached in all the world for a witness unto all nations; and then shall the end come. (Matthew 24:14)

In Numbers 14:21, the Lord declared, *But as truly as I live, all the earth shall be filled with the glory of the LORD.* This same promise became King David's final prayer. *Let the whole earth be filled with his glory; Amen, and Amen. The prayers of David the son of Jesse are ended.* (Psalm 72:19-20) The prophets established it as a proclamation as Isaiah and Habakkuk specifically echoed the original promise when they said that the knowledge of the Lord (or knowledge of the glory of the Lord) would fill the earth as the waters cover the sea. (Isaiah 11:9, Habakkuk 2:14) But the real fulfillment of God's plan is expressed most clearly in the New Living Translation of Isaiah's prophecy, *The earth will be filled with people who know the Lord.* When people through the whole earth know the Lord, the Great Commission will have been accomplished!

There is hope and assurance in our ministries that we can take His message and employ His method to complete His mission in our ministries. It is doable!

Appendix I

Lesson 1
God, the Creator
Genesis 1:24-28
Psalm 33:6-9, Isaiah 40:21-28, Colossians 1:16,
Hebrews 11:3, Revelation 4:11

Lesson 2
The Special Creation of People
Genesis 2:7, 2:18-22
Psalm 24:1, 100:3, 139:13-16;
Romans 8:38-39; Ephesians 5:28, 5:31

Lesson 3
Satan, the Deceiver
Genesis 3:1-6, 3:13-15
Mark 1:9-13, II Thessalonians 2:8-10,
I Peter 5:8, Revelation 12:9

Lesson 4
Adam and Eve Disobeyed God
Genesis 3:6-13, 3:16-19
Isaiah 59:2; Romans 3:23, 6:23;
James 1:13-15; I John 3:5

Lesson 5
The Chosen Family
Genesis 17:1-7, 17:15-19
Genesis 15:1-6, Isaiah 51:1-2, Galatians 3:16-18,
Hebrews 11:8-12, James 2:23

Lesson 6
God Tests Abraham
Genesis 22:2-13
Genesis 22:15-18, Romans 4:1-24, James 2:21-22

Lesson 7
There Will be Life after Death
Matthew 13:24-30, 13:37-43
Matthew 13:47-50, 25:31-46; Mark 9:47-48;
John 14:1-3; Philippians 3:20; I Thessalonians 4:13-18;
Revelation 20:12-15, 21:1-22:17

Lesson 8
Jesus Christ
Matthew 1:18-25
Matthew 16:13-20, 26:63-64; Luke 1:28-35;
John 1:1-14, 3:16; Philippians 2:5-11;
Colossians 1:15-20, 2:9

Lesson 9
God's Reconciliation Plan for Mankind
Matthew 27:27-38, 27:45, 27:50
Isaiah 53:5-6, Mark 10:45, John 1:29,
Ephesians 1:7, I Timothy 1:15, I Peter 2:24

Lesson 10
Jesus Conquered Death
Matthew 28:5-8
Acts 2:22-24; Romans 1:3-4, 8:33-34,
I Corinthians 15:12-22; I Peter 1:3

Lesson 11
What Must I Do to be Saved?
John 20:24-31
John 3:16-21; Acts 10:43, 16:25-31;
Romans 6:23, 10:9-10; Galatians 2:20, 3:1-29;
Ephesians 2:8-9; Hebrews 11:1-40

Lesson 12
How Do We Respond to God's Love?
Luke 19:1-10
Matthew 3:2, 4:17; Mark 1:15;
Luke 5:32, 13:15; Acts 2:31-41, 3:19-20

Lesson 13
I am a Friend of Jesus
John 14:8-9, 15:9-15
Matthew 7:16-20; John 14:15-23; Colossians 1:10;
II Peter 1:3-8; I John 4:7-8, 5:1-5

Lesson 14
Be Baptized
Acts 8:5-13
Acts 2:38, 18:8; Romans 6:4-5;
Galatians 3:27; Colossians 2:12

Lesson 15
We are the Light of the World
John 4:28-42
Mark 16:15-16; Luke 11:33-36; Acts 1:8

Lesson 16
Be Reconciled to Others
Matthew 18:23-35
Matthew 6:14; Mark 11:25-26; Luke 11:4, 17:3-4;
II Corinthians 2:5-11; Ephesians 4:32; Colossians 3:12-14

Lesson 17
Do Not Commit Adultery
II Samuel 12:1-9
Exodus 20:14, Proverbs 6:32,
I Corinthians 6:13-20, Ephesians 5:3-5, Colossians 3:1-11,
I Thessalonians 4:3-8, Hebrews 13:4

Lesson 18
Marriage is Sacred to God
Matthew 19:3-9
Genesis 2:20-24, I Corinthians 7:1-40, Ephesians 5:21-28

Lesson 19
Love Your Enemies
Luke 23:26-43
Mark 12:28-31, Luke 6:27-38,
John 13:34, Romans 12:17-21

Lesson 20
Responding to Injustice
Luke 22:47-53
Mark 12:28-31; Luke 6:32; John 4:7-8, 13:34;
Romans 12:17-21; I Corinthians 4:12; II Corinthians 12:10;
Ephesians 5:1-2; I Peter 1:22, 3:9; I John 3:11

Lesson 21
Give to Others
Matthew 25:32-46
Psalm 82:3, Proverbs 19:17, Proverbs 28:27,
Jeremiah 22:3, Matthew 5:42, Matthew 19:21

Lesson 22
Prayer
Acts 12:5-17
II Chronicles 7:14; Psalm 32:5-11, Jeremiah 29:12, 42:3;
Matthew 5:44, 7:11; I Thessalonians 5:17
Lesson 23
Store up Treasures in Heaven
John 12:1-8
Mark 8:34-38, Luke 12:32-34, I Corinthians 3:10-17,
I Timothy 6:17-19

Lesson 24
Do Not Worry
Mark 4:35-41
Proverbs 3:5-6, Luke 12:22-25, Galatians 2:20,
Hebrews 11:8-12, I Peter 1:21

Lesson 25
Do Not Judge Others
John 8:2-11
Luke 6:37, John 8:14-18, I Corinthians 4:3-5, James 4:12

Lesson 26
Ask, Seek, Knock
Luke 18:2-8
Ephesians 6:18; Colossians 4:12; Hebrews 4:16;
James 4:2-3, 5:16; I John 3:21-22, 5:14-15

Lesson 27
Worship in Every Place
Malachi 1:8-14
Isaiah 24:16, Isaiah 25:3, John 4:23-24

Lesson 28
Follow Christ, Part I
Matthew 19:16-22
Proverbs 3:5-6, Matthew 6:19-21, Romans 15:13,
I Thessalonians 1:3

Lesson 29
Follow Christ, Part II
Mark 2:13-17
Proverbs 19:17, Luke 15:1-31, Luke 19:10,
Galatians 6:9-10, James 3:18

Lesson 30
Tell Others About Jesus, Part I
Luke 5:1-11
Matthew 28:18-19, John 4:39-42, II Peter 3:9

Lesson 31
Tell Others About Jesus, Part II
Acts 16:9-15
Matthew 10:7-8, 28:19-20; Mark 16:15;
Romans 1:16-17; I Corinthians 2:1-5

Lesson 32
Tell Others About Jesus, Part III
Luke 10:1-9
Isaiah 6:8, Matthew 9:35-38,
John 4:35-38, Galatians 6:9-10

Lesson 33
Loving God, Part I
Luke 10:38-42
Matthew 11:28-30, Luke 6:47-49,
John 14:15, Philippians 2:12-13

Lesson 34
Loving God, Part II
John 10:7-14
Psalm 23:1-6, Psalm 100:1-5, Matthew 9:35-36

Lesson 35
Loving Others, Part I
Acts 4:29-35
Romans 12:3-21; I Corinthians 12:12-31, 14:26;
Ephesians 4:1-16

Lesson 36
Loving Others, Part II
Luke 10:30-37
Matthew 5:14-16; John 13:34-35; I Corinthians 13:1-13;
Ephesians 4:1-3; I John 3:16-18, 4:7-12

Lesson 37
Making Disciples, Part I
John 21:12-17
Matthew 28:19-20; Acts 20:28; I Corinthians 9:16-18;
I Thessalonians 5:11; II Timothy 2:2, 4:2-5

Lesson 38
Making Disciples, Part II
Matthew 28:16-20
John 14:15-17, Acts 2:42-47,
II Timothy 2:2, Hebrews 13:5-6

Lesson 39
Making Disciples, Part III
Acts 14:20-23
Acts 2:42-47, 11:25-30, 15:30-41, 18:23;
I Thessalonians 5:13-15

Lesson 40
God
Acts 17:22-31
Genesis 1:1, Deuteronomy 6:4-5, Mark 12:32,
I Timothy 2:5-6, Revelation 1:8

Lesson 41
Jesus
Matthew 17:1-8
John 1:1-5, 3:16; Philippians 2:5-11;
Colossians 1:15-20, 2:9; Hebrews 1:1-3

Lesson 42
The Holy Spirit
Acts 2:1-17
Luke 11:13, John 16:13, Acts 1:8,
I Corinthians 12:7-11, Galatians 5:16

Lesson 43
Love and Forgiveness
John 8:2-11
John 15:12-17, I John 2:8-11, 3:16, 4:1-21

Lesson 44
Justified Before God
Luke 18:10-14
Romans 3:24, 4:4-5, 4:25, 5:1-2, 5:8-10, 10:10;
James 2:20-26

Lesson 45
The Kingdom of God
John 3:1-8
John 18:36, Acts 1:3, Romans 6:4,
II Timothy 4:18, I Peter 1:23, II Peter 1:11

Lesson 46
The Bible
Matthew 4:1-11
Psalm 119, Romans 10:17, Ephesians 6:13-17,
II Peter 1:20-21, James 1:21

Lesson 47
The Church
Acts 6:1-7
Acts 2:42-47; 1 Corinthians 12:12-28;
Ephesians 2:19-21, 4:14-16; Hebrews 10:25

Lesson 48
Light of the World
Matthew 5:11-16
Matthew 5:1-7:29; II Corinthians 4:6; I John 1:7, 2:10

Lesson 49
Eternity
Luke 16:19-31
Matthew 19:16-26, 25:45-46; Romans 6:20-23;
I Thessalonians 4:13-18

Lesson 50
The Judge
John 5:21-30
Mark 9:41-48, I Corinthians 3:11-15,
II Corinthians 5:10, Revelation 20:11-15

Lesson 51
The Lord's Supper
I Corinthians 11:17-26
Luke 22:7-38, John 6:47-58,
I Corinthians 11:17-34, Revelation 19:9

Lesson 52
Baptism
Matthew 3:13-17
Matthew 28:16-20, Acts 8:26-40,
Romans 6:3-13, Colossians 2:9-12

Lesson 53
If You Love God, You Will Obey
Matthew 7:24-27
Matthew 4:4, Hebrews 4:12, James 1:22-24

Lesson 54
Love
Luke 10:30-37
John 13:34-35, I John 4:7-12

Lesson 55
Faith
Mark 6:34-44
Matthew 14:22-33

Lesson 56
The Bible
Matthew 4:1-11
Matthew 5:17-19, Romans 1:16,
II Peter 1:21, Hebrews 4:12,

Lesson 57
Telling The Story
Matthew 28:16-20
Mark 16:15-18, Luke 24:46-49, Acts 1:8

Lesson 58
Jesus Christ
Matthew 1:18-25
John 14:1-14, Philippians 2:5-11, Colossians 1:13-20

Lesson 59
Water Baptism
Matthew 3:13-17
Acts 2:38, 8:36; Romans 6:3-13; Colossians 2:12

Lesson 60
Daily Time with God
Luke 10:38-42
Matthew 5:17, Luke 6:12, John 4:24

Lesson 61
Church
Acts 6:1-7
Acts 2:46-47

Lesson 62
Obedience
Matthew 26:36-46
Luke 22:41-44, Hebrews 5:8

Lesson 63
Expressing Adoration
Revelation 5:8-14
Ephesians 5:19-20, Colossians 3:16,
Hebrews 2:12, James 5:13

132

Lesson 64
Giving
Luke 18:18-23
Mark 12:41-44

Lesson 65
Expressing Thankfulness
Luke 17:11-19
Philippians 4:6; Colossians 2:7, 4:2

Lesson 66
The Kingdom of God
Luke 8:26-37
Matthew 6:10, 6:33, 12:24-28; Luke 12:32

Lesson 67
Redemption
Luke 27:33-43
Ephesians 3:19-21

Lesson 68
The Resurrection
John 20:1-18
John 5:29, 11:25

Lesson 69
The Trinity
John 14:8-28
Matthew 28:19

Lesson 70
Demons
Matthew 17:14-21
Mark 16:17-20, Colossians 2:15

Lesson 71
Angels
Acts 12:1-11
Luke 4:10; Colossians 2:18; Hebrews 1:7, 12:22, 13:2

Lesson 72
Power Evangelism
Acts 2:1-8
Acts 2:38-41, 2:46-47; I Corinthians 12:7-11, 13:1-3

Lesson 73
New People Doing New Things
Acts 3:1-10
Luke 24:46-49, Acts 1:8, 3:19-21, 3:26, 4:4

Lesson 74
Divine Correction
Acts 5:1-11
John 14:17, 15:26, 16:8-15;
I Peter 1:22; I John 4:6, 5:6

Lesson 75
Wisdom to Lead
Acts 6:1-7
Acts 13:1-2, 15:1-41; I Timothy 3:1-13;
Titus 1:5-9; James 1:5

Lesson 76
Boldness in the Face of Adversity
Acts 6:8-15
Matthew 5:11-12, 10:19, 24:9;
Mark 13:11; John 15:18-23; Acts 7:1-54

Lesson 77
Getting Rid of Witchcraft
Acts 8:9-13, 8:18-24
Matthew 9:34, 12:24-31; Luke 11:15-26;
Acts 13:6-12, 14:8-18,16:16-18;
I Corinthians 10:20-22, 12:2-3; I Timothy 4:1

Lesson 78
Reaching Out to All Men
Acts 10:44-48
John 3:16-17, Acts 10:1-43, 11:1-18;
I Corinthians 12:13; Galatians 3:28; Ephesians 6:8-9;
Colossians 3:11, 3:25; I Timothy 2:4;
James 2:1-9; II Peter 3:9

Lesson 79
The Praying Church
Acts 12:5-17
Matthew 6:6-13, 21:21-22; Luke 18:1-8;
John 14:13-14, 16:23-24; Romans 12:10-15;
I Corinthians 14:14-15; II Corinthians 1:11;
Philippians 1:19, 4:6; Colossians 4:2-3;
I Timothy 2:1-3; James 5:15-16; I John 5:14-15

Lesson 80
Appointing Leadership
Acts 12:25-13:5
Matthew 10:1-8; Mark 3:13-15, 6:7; Luke 9:1-2;
Acts 6:3; I Timothy 3:8-13, 5:1-2, 5:17

Lesson 81
Confronting Conflict
Acts 15:6-22
Matthew 18:15-20, 18:21-22; Luke 17:1-4;
Acts 15:1-41; Romans 16:17-18;
I Corinthians 1:10, 3:3, 5:11-13;
Galatians 2:11-14; Titus 5:1

Lesson 82
Hearing The Voice of God
Acts 16:6-10
Matthew 13:9-17; Luke 8:18; John 12:28-30; Acts 2:17;
Hebrews 1:1-2, 2:4; Revelation 2:7, 2:11, 2:17,
2:29, 3:6, 3:13, 3:22, 13:9, 14:6-7, 22:6

Lesson 83
Rejoicing in the Face of Trouble
Acts 16:25-34
Matthew 5:11-12; Luke 6:22-23; Acts 16:16-40;
Romans 5:2-5; Colossians 1:24, James 1:2-4;
I Peter 1:6-9, 4:13

Lesson 84
Doing God's Will
Acts 21:10-14
Mark 3:35; Acts 9:15-16, 18:21;
Romans 1:10, 8:27, 12:2, 15:32; I Corinthians 1:1;
II Corinthians 8:5; Ephesians 1:1, 1:9, 6:6;
Colossians 1:1, 4:12; I Thessalonians 4:3, 5:18;
II Timothy 1:1; Hebrews 2:4, 10:36; I Peter 3:17, 4:2, 4:19; II
Peter 1:21; II John 2:17

Lesson 85
Fruit of Love
Ruth 1:6-18
Matthew 5:43-46, 22:36-40; Luke 6:27-32;
John 13:34-35; Galatians 5:13-14, 5:22-23;
I John 3:11-19, 4:7-13

Lesson 86
Fruit of Joy
Acts 5:27-42
Luke 2:8-11; John 16:20-22, 17:12-16;
Acts 13:50-52, 20:22-24; Romans 5:8-11, 14:16-18;
II Corinthians 8:1-2; Galatians 5:22-23;
I Thessalonians 1:6; Hebrews 12:2-3; James 1:2-4;
I Peter 1:6-8, 1:12-14; I John 1:3-4; Jude 24-25

Lesson 87
Fruit of Peace
II Kings 6:15-23
Mark 5:34; Luke 1:76-79, 10:5, 19:37-38;
John 16:33, 20:21; Romans 2:10, Romans 5:1-5,
Romans 8:5-6, 14:17-19, 15:13; II Corinthians 13:11; Galatians
5:22-23; Ephesians 2:14-18;
Philippians 4:4-9; Colossians 1:20; I Thessalonians 5:23,

Lesson 88
Fruit of Longsuffering
Luke 15:12-24
Romans 2:1-4; II Corinthians 6:4-10; Galatians 5:22-23;
Ephesians 4:1-3; Colossians 1:9-12, 3:12-14;
I Timothy 1:16; II Timothy 3:10-11, 4:2;
I Peter 3:18-20; II Peter 3:9-18

Lesson 89
Fruit of Gentleness
Philemon 1:1-25
II Corinthians 10:1-3, Galatians 5:22-23,
I Thessalonians 2:1-12, I Timothy 2:24-26, Titus 3:1-4

Lesson 90
Fruit of Goodness
Genesis 50:15-21
Luke 6:28, Romans 2:1-4, 11:16-25, 12:14, 12:19-21, 15:14;
Galatians 5:22-23; Ephesians 5:9-10; I Thessalonians 5:15; II
Thessalonians 1:11-12

Lesson 91
Fruit of Faith
Acts 3:11-18
Romans 4:16-21, 10:6-17, 12:3-8; Galatians 5:22-23; Hebrews
11:1-40; James 2:14-26, 5:14-16

Lesson 92
Fruit of Meekness
Matthew 26: 47-55
Matthew 5:5, 11:29, 21:5; I Corinthians 4:21;
II Corinthians 10:1-3; Galatians 5:22-23, 6:1;
Ephesians 4:1-3; Colossians 3:12-13; I Timothy 6:11;
II Timothy 2:25, Titus 3:1-2, James 1:21, 3:13;
I Peter 3:1-4, 3:15

Lesson 93
Fruit of Temperance
II Samuel 11:6-11
Matthew 5:28; Mark 4:19; Romans 6:12, 13:14;
I Corinthians 8:4-13, 10:23-33; Galatians 5:22-23; Ephesians
4:22; I Thessalonians 4:4-5, I Timothy 6:6-10;
II Timothy 2:22, 4:3; Titus 2:11-15, 3:3; James 1:13-15, 4:2; I
Peter 2:11, 4:1-6; II Peter 1:5-7; I John 2:16-17

Lesson 94
Follow Me
Luke 9: 57-6
Isaiah 51:1; Hosea 6:3; Matthew 4:19, 16:24, 19:21;
Luke 18:18-22; John 10:1-5, 10:27, 21:21-22;
Romans 14:19; I Corinthians 14:1; Philippians 3:12;
I Thessalonians 5:15; II Timothy 2:22;
Hebrews 12:14, 13:7; III John 1:11

Lesson 95
Repent
Acts 9:1-9
Matthew 4:17; Luke 17:3-4;
Acts 2:38, 3:19, 8:22, 17:30, 26:20;
Revelation 2:5, 3:3, 3:19

Lesson 96
Rejoice
Luke 15:4-10
Matthew 5:12; Romans 5:2;
Philippians 1:18, 2:18, 3:1, 4:4;
Colossians 1:24; I Thessalonians 5:16;
James 1:9; I Peter 1:8, 4:13

Lesson 97
Let Your Light Shine
Genesis 13: 5-12
Matthew 5:16, 13:43; Philippians 2:14-16;
Ephesians 4:1-32; Colossians 1:10; I Thessalonians 2:12

Lesson 98
Honor God's Law
Exodus 19:17-20, 20:1-17
Matthew 5:17-18, 15:1-6, 22:35-40, 23:23;
Mark 10:19-21; Romans 3:19-28;
Galatians 3:19-25; Ephesians 2:8-9

Lesson 99
Be Reconciled
Genesis 33:1-11
Matthew 5:24–25, Galatians 6:1-2,
II Corinthians 5:18-20, II Thessalonians 3:14-15

Lesson 100
Practice Truthfulness
Judges 16:4-6, 15-21
Psalm 15:1-2; Proverbs 19:5, 23:23; Matthew 5:37;
John 14:16-17, 15:26, 16:13; Ephesians 4:15, 4:29; Revelation 21:8

Lesson 101
Be Perfect
I Kings 11:1-6
Genesis 6:9, 17:1; Deuteronomy 18:13;
II Samuel 22:33; I Kings 8:61, 11:4, 15:3, 15:14;
II Kings 20:3; I Chronicles 12:38, 28:9, 29:9, 29:19;
II Chronicles 15:17, 16:9, 19:9, 25:2; Job 1:1, 1:8, 2:3, 8:20;
Psalm 18:32, 37:37, 64:4, 101:2, 101:6;
Proverbs 2:21, 11:5; Isaiah 38:3; Matthew 5:48, 19:21; Luke
6:40; I Corinthians 2:6

Lesson 102
Go the Second Mile
II Samuel 9: 3-13
Ecclesiastes 4:9; Amos 3:3; Matthew 5:38-42;
Luke 6:27-36; Romans 14:19; I Corinthians 10:24;
Galatians 6:2; Ephesians 4:28; I Thessalonians 5:11

Lesson 103
Practice Self-control
II Samuel 11:1-5
Matthew 5:27-30; Mark 10:19-21; Romans 1:28-32;
I Corinthians 6:12-20, 7:2-5; Galatians 5:16-26;
Ephesians 5:3-7; Colossians 3:5-6,
I Thessalonians 4:3-4; II Peter 2:9-10

Lesson 104
Practice Secret Disciplines
Luke 8:41-42, 49-56
Matthew 6:1-18, 8:1-4; Mark 7:31-36; Luke 5:12-14

Lesson 105
Lay up Treasures in Heaven
Acts 4: 32-37
Proverbs 15:6; Matthew 6:19-21, 13:44-46, 19:16-22;
Mark 10:17-22; Luke 12:13-21, 12:22-34, 18:18-23;
I Timothy 6:6-19; Hebrews 24:26; James 2:5;
Revelation 3:17-18

Lesson 106
Take Initiative to Seek God's Kingdom
Luke 12: 24-34
II Chronicles 12:14, 15:12-13; Matthew 6:33, 7:7-12;
Luke 11:9-13, 13:24; Acts 15:17, 17:27-28;
Romans 2:6-7; Colossians 3:1-2; Hebrews 11:6

Lesson 107
Judge Not
Genesis 38: 3-11
Matthew 7:1-6; Luke 6:37-39;
John 5:30, 7:24, 8:15-16, 8:26, 12:47-48; Acts 23:3;
Romans 14:1-13; I Corinthians 4:1-5, 5:12-6:4, 11:27-34

Lesson 108
Discretion
Acts 13: 6-12
Psalm 92:6, 94:8; Proverbs 12:1, 30:2-3;
Isaiah 19:11; Jeremiah 10:6-8, 10:14, 10:21, 51:17; Matthew
7:6; II Peter 2:12; Jude 10

Lesson 109
Take on Christ's Yoke
Mark 6:7-13
Matthew 11:29-30

Lesson 110
Resourcefulness
I Samuel 1:9-20
Matthew 7:7-11, 18:19, 21:21-22; Luke 11:9-13;
John 14:12-14, 15:7, 15:16, 16:23-27; Ephesians 3:20; James
1:5-6, 4:2-3; I John 3:21-22, 5:14-15

Lesson 111
Sensitivity
I Samuel 20:1-17
Matthew 5:43-48, 7:12; Luke 6:27-36;
I Corinthians 13:3-8; Galatians 5:22-23;
Ephesians 4:25-5:2; Colossians 3:12-17;
I Thessalonians 5:15; James 215-16;
II Peter 1:5-7; I John 4:20-21

Lesson 112
Pray for Laborers
Matthew 20:1-16
Psalm 126:5; Proverbs 10:5; Ecclesiastes 11:4;
Jeremiah 23:2-4; Matthew 9:38; John 4:35-38;
Ephesians 6:18-20; Colossians 4:3-4

Lesson 113
Choosing the Narrow Road
Judges 14:1-3
Deuteronomy 30:15-20; Joshua 24:14-16; I Kings 18:21;
Matthew 7:13-14; Romans 6:1-14, 7:15-25;
II Corinthians 5:17-19; Galatians 5:16-25;
Ephesians 4:17-32; Colossians 3:1-17

Lesson 114
Deny Yourself
Acts 9:10-19
Matthew 10:38; Mark 8:34; Luke 9:23, 9:62

Lesson 115
Beware of False Prophets
I Kings 22:2-5, 13-18, 26-28, 35-37
Jeremiah 14:14; Lamentations 2:14;
Matthew 7:15, 24:11, 24:23-24; Mark 13:21-22;
Luke 6:26; I Timothy 4:1-3; II Timothy 3:1-9, 4:1-5;
II Peter 2:1-22; I John 4:1-3; Jude 1:5-19

Lesson 116
Be Wise as Serpents
Acts 23: 6-10
Proverbs 3:13, 3:21, 4:5, 4:7, 5:1, 9:10,
16:16, 19:8, 23:23; Matthew 10:16,

Lesson 117
Fear God, Not Man
John 19:1-11
Psalm 19:9, 34:11, 111:10;
Proverbs 1:7, 1:29, 2:5, 8:13, 9:10, 10:27,
14:26, 14:27, 15:16, 15:33, 16:6, 19:23, 22:4;
Matthew 10:26,

Lesson 118
Attentiveness to God's Voice
Matthew 11:15
Deuteronomy 15:5, 28:2, 28:15, 30:10;
Acts 27:1, 27:5-6, 27:9-11, 27:14, 27:21-24, 27:42-44

Lesson 119
Honor Parents
Matthew 21: 28-32
Exodus 20:12; Deuteronomy 5:16;
Matthew 15:4, 15:4-6, 19:19; Mark 7:10, 10:19;
Luke 18:20; Ephesians 6:1-2; Colossians 3:20

Lesson 120
Beware of Religious Leaven
John 9: 8-34
Matthew 16:6, 6:2, 6:5, 6:16, 15:7, 16:3, 22:18, 23:13-15,
23:23-29, 24:51; Mark 7:6; Luke 11:44, 12:56

Lesson 121
Go to Those Who Offend You
Genesis 21:25-34
Matthew 5:23-24, 5:25-26, 18:15-20;
Luke 12:57-59; Acts 15:1-35, 15:36-41;
Galatians 2:11; II Timothy 4:11; Philemon 1:1-15;
James 5:16; I John 5:16

Lesson 122
Beware of Covetousness
I Kings 21:1-16
Luke 12:13-21, 18:18-23; Romans 7:7-12, 13:8-10;
I Corinthians 5:11, 6:9-11; Ephesians 5:5;
I Timothy 3:1-13, 6:6-11; II Timothy 3:1-5;
Titus 1:6-12; I Peter 5:2; II Peter 2:14

Lesson 123
Love the Lord
II Samuel 24: 18-25
Matthew 6:24, 22:34-40; Mark 12:28-34;
Luke 10:25-28, 11:42, 16:13; Romans 8:26-28;
I Corinthians 8:3; I John 4:10, 4:20, 5:2

Lesson 124
Forgive Offenders
Acts 7:54-60
Matthew 6:14-15, 18:21, 18:21-35; Mark 11:24-26;
Luke 6:37-38, 17:3, 17:1-4; II Corinthians 2:3-11

Lesson 125
Despise Not the Little Ones
I Samuel 3:1-15
Matthew 18:6-10, Mark 9:42, Luke 17:2

Lesson 126
Honor Marriage
Genesis 20:1-18
Matthew 5:27-32, 19:1-12; I Corinthians 7:1-16;
Ephesians 5:22-33; Hebrews 13:4

Lesson 127
Be Servants
John 13:1-17
Matthew 20:26-28, 23:8-12; Mark 9:33-37, 10:35-45;
Luke 22:24-30; I Corinthians 8:1-13, 9:19-23;
Galatians 5:13-14; Philippians 2:5-11

Lesson 128
Receive the Lord's Body and Blood
Matthew 26:17-30
Matthew 26:26-30, Mark 14:22-26, Luke 22:14-20,
John 6:22-58, I Corinthians 11: 17-34

Lesson 129
Make the Temple a House of Prayer
Matthew 8:5-13
Isaiah 2:2-4, 56:6-8, 60:1-7; Micah 4:1-3;
Matthew 21:12-16; Mark 11:15-18; Luke 19:45-48;
Revelation 5:9-13

Lesson 130
Ask in Faith
Matthew 15:21-28
Matthew 21:21-22, 17:14-21; Acts 3:11-16, 14:8-10,
15:7-9; Romans 1:16-17, 4:13-21, 10:17, 12:3;
I Corinthians 2:4-5; II Corinthians 5:7;
II Thessalonians 1:3-11; Hebrews 6:12, 11:1-12:2;
James 1:5-8, 2:14-18, 5:14-15

Lesson 131
Bring in the Poor
Luke 14:7-24
Matthew 11:2-5, 19:16-22; Mark 10:17-22;
Luke 4:18-19, 6:20-23, 6:30-36, 7:20-23, 14:12-14,
18:18-23, 19:1-10; Acts 11:27-30; Romans 12:9-21,
15:25-27; II Corinthians 9:1-9; Galatians 2:9-10; Philippians
4:10-19; James 2:1-5

Lesson 132
Give to Caesar What Belongs to Him
Matthew 22:15-22
Matthew 22:19-21, 8:5-13, 17:24-27;
Luke 2:1-5, 7:1-9, 20:20-26; Romans 13:1-7;
I Timothy 2:1-3; Hebrews 13:7, 13:17; I Peter 2:13-17

Lesson 133
Love Your Neighbor
Ruth 2:1-9
Matthew 5:43-48, 19:16-22, 22:34-40; Mark 12:28-34; Luke
10:27-37; Romans 13:8-10, 15:1-6;
Galatians 5:13-15; Ephesians 4:25;
James 2:14-16; I John 4:7-19

Lesson 134
Anticipate the Lord's Return
Luke 12:35-48
Matthew 24:42-44; I Corinthians 15:35-58;
Colossians 3:1-4; I Thessalonians 4:13-5:11;
II Timothy 4:8; Titus 2:11-14; I Peter 1:3-5, 3:15;
I John 3:2-3

Lesson 135
Be Born Again
John 3:9-21
John 3:1-21; Romans 6:1-14; II Corinthians 5:14-21;
Colossians 2:11-14, 3:1-5;
I Peter 1:23; I John 5:4-5

Lesson 136
Keep the Lord's Commands
Matthew 5:1-3, 17-28
John 12:49-50, 13:34-35, 14:15-16, 14:21, 15:12-17;
I John 2:3-11, 3:22-5:5

Lesson 137
Watch and Pray
Acts 9:36-42
Matthew 26:41, 6:5-13, 17:14-21, 21:21-22;
Mark 11:22-26; Luke 6:28, 11:1-4, 18:1-8; Acts 6:3-4; Romans
8:26-28, 12:12, 15:30; Ephesians 6:18;
Philippians 4:6; I Thessalonians 5:16-18;
I Timothy 2:1-3, 2:8; James 5:14-15; I Peter 4:7;
Jude 1:20; Revelation 5:8

Lesson 138
Feed the Lord's Sheep
John 10:1-6, 14-18
Isaiah 40:11; Jeremiah 23:4, 31:10, Ezekiel 34:5-12; Matthew
9:36, 26:31; Mark 6:34, 14:27; John 10:1-28, 21:15-16;
Hebrews 13:20-21; I Peter 2:25, 5:1-4

Lesson 139
Baptize Disciples
Acts 8: 26-38
Matthew 28:19, Romans 6:3-14, I Corinthians 12:12-14,
Galatians 3:26-29, Ephesians 4:4-6, Colossians 2:11-14,
I Peter 3:21-22

Lesson 140
Receive God's Power
Acts 4:23-31
Mark 16:15-20; Luke 24: 46-49; John 20:19-22;
Acts 1:8, 2:1-4, 8:14-18, 9:1-19, 10:1-48, 19:1-10; Ephesians
5:18

Lesson 141
Making Disciples
Acts 16:1-5
Matthew 28:20; Acts 18:24-27;
I Corinthians 1:10-13, 4:15, 11:1;
II Timothy 2:2; Titus 2:1-10

Lesson 142
Alert Servants
Mark 13:33-37
Matthew 24:43, Luke 12:39, I Thessalonians 5:2-4,
II Peter 3:10, Revelation 16:15

Lesson 143
Budding Fig Tree
Matthew 24:32-35
Mark 13:28-32, Luke 21:29-33

Lesson 144
Barren Fig Tree
Luke 13:6-9
Psalm 1:1-3, 92:13-14; Proverbs 11:30;
Matthew 7:18-19, 12:33; Mark 4:28; John 15:2-16

Lesson 145
Children in the Market
Matthew 11:16-19
Matthew 12:22-32, Luke 7:31-35, John 10:20-21
Lesson 146
Dinner Guests
Luke 14:15-24
Matthew 22:2-8, Revelation 19:9

Lesson 147
Divided Kingdom
Matthew 12:24-30
Matthew 9:4, 9:34; Mark 3:22-27;
Luke 11:14-23; John 2:25

Lesson 148
Friend at Midnight
Luke 11:5-13
Matthew 6:8, 7:7, 21:22; Mark 11:24;
John 15:7; James 1:6; I John 3:22

Lesson 149
Good Samaritan
Luke 10:25-37
Deuteronomy 6:5; Matthew 5:44;
Luke 6:27, 6:35; John 4:9

Lesson 150
Good Shepherd
John 10:1-18
Psalm 23:1; Matthew 9:36, Mark 6:34;
Hebrews 13:20; I Peter 2:25, 5:4

Lesson 151
Great Physical
Matthew 9:10-13
, Exodus 15:26,
Deuteronomy 7:15; Psalm 103:3; Matthew 4:24;
Mark 2:15-17; Luke 4:40, 5:29-32, 6:17

Lesson 152
The Groom's Attendants
Matthew 9:14-15
Psalm 19:5, Isaiah 61:10,
Mark 2:18-20, Luke 5:33-25, John 3:29

Lesson 153
The Growing Seed
Mark 4:26-29
Matthew 13:19-43

Lesson 154
The Humbled Guest
Luke 14:7-11
Isaiah 61:3, Revelation 6:11, 7:9, 7:13

Lesson 155
Laborers in the Vineyard
Matthew 20:1-16
Matthew 19:30, 22:14; Luke 3:14;
Philippians 4:11; I Timothy 6:6-10; Hebrews 13:5

Lesson 156
Pearl of Great Price
Matthew 13:45-46
Proverbs 2:4, 3:14-15, 8:10,19

Lesson 157
The Landowner
Matthew 21:33-46
Matthew 5:12,
Matthew 23:34, 23:37, 26:3, 27:1; Mark 12:1-12;
Luke 20:9-18; John 11:53; Acts 4:27, 7:52;
I Thessalonians 2:15; Hebrews 1:2, 11:36-37

Lesson 158
The Lost Sheep
Luke 15:4-7
Psalm 95:7, 100:3, 119:176;
Jeremiah 50:6; Ezekiel 34:11-12

Lesson 159
The Marriage Feast
Matthew 22:1-14
Ephesians 5:25-32, Revelation 19:7-9

Lesson 160
The Mustard Seed
Matthew 13:31-32
Mark 4:30-32, Luke 13:18-19

Lesson 161
Net of Fish
Matthew 13:47-50
Matthew 13:42, 22:10, 25:32

150

Lesson 162
The Pharisee and the Publican
Luke 18:9-14
Psalm 10:2, 10:4; Proverbs 8:13, 11:2, 13:10, 16:18, 29:23

Lesson 163
The Prodigal Son
Luke 15:11-32
II Chronicles 7:14, 34:27; Psalm 9:12, 10:17, 34:2, 69:32;
Proverbs 29:23; Isaiah 57:15; Matthew 23:12;
James 4:6; I Peter 5:6

Lesson 164
Ten Minas
Luke 19:11-27
Matthew 25:14-30, John 1:11

Lesson 165
The Rich Man and Lazarus
Luke 16:19-31
Proverbs 28:6, 28:11; Jeremiah 9:23;
Matthew 19:23; Luke 1:53, 6:24; I Timothy 6:9, 6:17; James
2:6, 5:1; Revelation 3:17

Lesson 166
The Rich Fool
Luke 12:16-21
Proverbs 28:6, 28:11; Jeremiah 9:23; Matthew 19:23;
Luke 1:53, 6:24; I Timothy 6:9, 6:17; James 2:6, 5:1;
Revelation 3:17

Lesson 167
The Servant's Duties
Luke 17:7-10
Romans 4:6, Ephesians 2:9, Titus 3:5, Philemon 1:11

Lesson 174
Two Sons
Matthew 21:28-32
Luke 13:29-30

Lesson 175
The Unclean Spirit
Matthew 12:43-45
Matthew 19:30, 20:16;
Mark 10:31; Luke 11:24-26

Lesson 176
The Unjust Judge
Luke 18:1-8
II Chronicles 16:9, Isaiah 65:24, Matthew 6:8,
John 3:16, Romans 8:32, Ephesians 5:25

Lesson 177
The Unjust Steward
Luke 16:1-13
Matthew 6:129-24, 25:21;
Luke 19:17, I Corinthians 4:2

Lesson 178
The Unmerciful Servant
Matthew 18:21-35
Psalm 18:25; Matthew 5:7, 7:12; Luke 6:36

Lesson 179
The Unprepared Builder
Luke 14:28-30
Proverbs 3:5-6,14:12, 16:25, 24:27

Lesson 180
The Vine and Branches
John 15:1-17
Matthew 3:10, 5:16, 7:19, 12:50, 15:13, 17:13;
John 10:11-15; Romans 5:7-8; Philippians 1:11;
Colossians 1:6; I John 2:6, 3:16

Lesson 181
The Wise Servant
Matthew 24:45-51
Matthew 8:12, 25:21-23, 25:30;
Luke 12:42-48; I Corinthians 4:2

Lesson 182
Watching Servants
Luke 12:35-40
Matthew 24:43-44, 25:1, 25:13; Mark 13:33;
Luke 21:34-36; Ephesians 6:14; I Thessalonians 5:2, 5:6;
I Peter 1:13, II Peter 3:10; Revelation 3:3, 16:1, 16:15

Lesson 183
The Wise Builder
Matthew 7:24-27
Luke 6:46-49, Romans 15:20,
I Corinthians 3:10-11, Ephesians 2:20,
I Timothy 6:19, Hebrews 6:1

Appendix II

Matthew 16:21
Matthew 17:12
Matthew 17:15
Matthew 27:19
Mark 5:26
Mark 8:31
Mark 9:12
Luke 9:22
Luke 13:2
Luke 17:25
Luke 22:15
Luke 24:26
Luke 24:46
Acts 1:3
Acts 3:18
Acts 9:16
Acts 17:3
Acts 28:5
Romans 8:18
I Corinthians 12:26
II Corinthians 1:5
II Corinthians 1:6
II Corinthians 1:7
Galatians 3:4
Philippians 1:29
Colossians 1:24
I Thessalonians 2:14
II Thessalonians 1:5
II Timothy 1:12
II Timothy 3:11
Hebrews 2:9
Hebrews 2:10
Hebrews 2:18
Hebrews 5:8
Hebrews 9:26

Hebrews 10:32
Hebrews 13:12
I Peter 1:11
I Peter 2:20
I Peter 2:21
I Peter 2:23
I Peter 3:14
I Peter 3:17
I Peter 3:18
I Peter 4:1
I Peter 4:13
I Peter 4:15
I Peter 4:19
I Peter 5:1
I Peter 5:9
I Peter 5:10
Revelation 2:10

Appendix III

Psalm 90:7 – *We are burned up by the heat of your passion, and troubled by your wrath.* (BBE)

Isaiah 10:25 – For in a very short time my passion will be over, and my wrath will be turned to their destruction. (BBE)

Isaiah 14:6 – *He whose rod was on the peoples with an unending wrath, ruling the nations in passion, with an uncontrolled rule.* (BBE)

Ezekiel 22:20 – *As they put silver and brass and iron and lead and tin together inside the oven, heating up the fire on it to make it soft; so will I get you together in my wrath and in my passion, and, heating the fire with my breath, will make you soft.* (BBE)

Ezekiel 22:22 – *As silver becomes soft in the oven, so you will become soft in it; and you will be certain that I the Lord have let loose my passion on you.* (BBE)

Ezekiel 22:31 – *And I let loose my passion on them, and have put an end to them in the fire of my wrath: I have made the punishment of their ways come on their heads, says the Lord.* (BBE)

Ezekiel 24:13 – *As for your unclean purpose: because I have been attempting to make you clean, but you have not been made clean from it, you will not be made clean till I have let loose my passion on you in full measure.* (BBE)

Acts 26:11 – *And I gave them punishment frequently, in all the Synagogues, forcing them to say things against God; and burning with passion exceedingly* (*mad* – KJV) *against them, I went after them even into far-away towns.* (BBE)

Ephesians 4:31 – *Banish from among you all bitterness and passion and anger and clamor and slander, as well as all malice.* (MNT)

Colossians 3:8 – *But now you also must renounce them all. Anger, passion, and ill-will must be put away; slander, too, and foul talk, so that they may never soil your lips.* (MNT)

Titus 1:7 – *For the overseer must be free from all charge [against him] as God's steward; not headstrong (not over-fond of having his own way* – WNT), *not passionate (soon angry* – KJV) (*not a man of a passionate temper* – WNT), *not disorderly through wine (nor a hard drinker* – WNT), *not a striker, not seeking gain by base means.* (DBY)

Appendix IV

Numbers 5:14 – *And the spirit of jealousy come upon him, and he be jealous of his wife, and she be defiled: or if the spirit of jealousy come upon him, and he be jealous of his wife, and she be not defiled.*

Numbers 5:30 – *Or when the spirit of jealousy cometh upon him, and he be jealous over his wife, and shall set the woman before the LORD, and the priest shall execute upon her all this law.*

Deuteronomy 32:16 – *They provoked him to jealousy with strange gods, with abominations provoked they him to anger.*

Deuteronomy 32:21 – *They have moved me to jealousy with that which is not God; they have provoked me to anger with their vanities: and I will move them to jealousy with those which are not a people; I will provoke them to anger with a foolish nation.*

I Kings 14:22 – *And Judah did evil in the sight of the LORD, and they provoked him to jealousy with their sins which they had committed, above all that their fathers had done.*

I Kings 19:10 – *And he said, I have been very jealous for the LORD God of hosts: for the children of Israel have forsaken thy covenant, thrown down thine altars, and slain thy prophets with the sword; and I, even I only, am left; and they seek my life, to take it away.*

I Kings 19:14 – *And he said, I have been very jealous for the LORD God of hosts: because the children of Israel have forsaken thy covenant, thrown down thine altars, and slain thy prophets with the sword; and I, even I only, am left; and they seek my life, to take it away.*

Psalm 78:58 – *For they provoked him to anger with their high places, and moved him to jealousy with their graven images.*

Ezekiel 39:25 – *Therefore thus saith the Lord GOD; Now will I bring again the captivity of Jacob, and have mercy upon the whole house of Israel, and will be jealous for my holy name.*

Joel 2:18 – *Then will the LORD be jealous for his land, and pity his people.*

Zechariah 1:14 – *So the angel that communed with me said unto me, Cry thou, saying, Thus saith the LORD of hosts; I am jealous for Jerusalem and for Zion with a great jealousy.*

Zechariah 8:2 – *Thus saith the LORD of hosts; I was jealous for Zion with great jealousy, and I was jealous for her with great fury.*

Genesis 26:14 – *For he had possession of flocks, and possession of herds, and great store of servants: and the Philistines envied him.*

Genesis 30:1 – *And when Rachel saw that she bare Jacob no children, Rachel envied her sister; and said unto Jacob, Give me children, or else I die.*

Genesis 37:11 – *And his brethren envied him; but his father observed the saying.*

Numbers 11:29 – *And Moses said unto him, Enviest thou for my sake? would God that all the LORD'S people were prophets, and that the LORD would put his spirit upon them!*

Psalm 37:1 – *Fret not thyself because of evildoers, neither be thou envious against the workers of iniquity.*

Psalm 73:3 – *For I was envious at the foolish, when I saw the prosperity of the wicked.*

Psalm 106:16 – *They envied Moses also in the camp, and Aaron the saint of the LORD.*

Proverbs 3:31 – *Envy thou not the oppressor, and choose none of his ways.*

Proverbs 5:19 – *As a loving hind and a gentle doe, let her breasts ever give you rapture; let your passion at all times be moved by her love.* (BBE)

Proverbs 23:17 – *Let not thine heart envy sinners: but be thou in the fear of the LORD all the day long.*

Proverbs 24:1 – *Be not thou envious against evil men, neither desire to be with them.*

Proverbs 24:19 – *Fret not thyself because of evil men, neither be thou envious at the wicked.*

Isaiah 11:13 – *The envy also of Ephraim shall depart, and the adversaries of Judah shall be cut off: Ephraim shall not envy Judah, and Judah shall not vex Ephraim.*

Ezekiel 31:9 – *I have made him fair by the multitude of his branches: so that all the trees of Eden, that were in the garden of God, envied him.*

Romans 1:26 – *That is why God has given them up to passions of dishonor; for on the one hand their women actually changed the natural function of sex into that which is against nature.* (MNT)

Romans 1:27 – *and on the other hand their men likewise abandoned the natural use of women, and were ablaze with passion for one another; men with men practising shameless acts and receiving in their own person that recompense of their wrong-doing which necessarily followed.* (MNT)

Romans 7:5 – *For whilst we were under the thraldom of our earthly natures, sinful passions (motions of sins – KJV) – made sinful by the Law – were always being aroused to action in our bodily faculties that they might yield fruit to death.* (WNT, also MNT, TCNT, & DBY)

I Corinthians 7:9 – *If, however, they are not exercising self-control, by all means let them marry; for marriage is better than the fever of passion.* (MNT)

Galatians 5:24 – *And those who belong to Christ have crucified the flesh with its passions (affections – KJV) and appetites.* (MNT, also ASV)

Ephesians 2:3 – *And among them we all once passed our lives, indulging the passions of our flesh, carrying out the dictates of our senses and temperament, and were by nature the children of wrath like all the rest.* (MNT)

Ephesians 4:19 – *Who having no more power of feeling, have given themselves up to evil passions, to do all unclean things with overmuch desire.* (BBE)

Ephesians 4:22 – *For you learned with regard to your former way of living that you must cast off your old nature, which, yielding to deluding passions, grows corrupt.* (TCNT)

Ephesians 5:5 – *Being certain of this, that no man who gives way to the passions of the flesh, no unclean person, or one who has desire for the property of others, or who gives worship to images, has any heritage in the kingdom of Christ and God.* (BBE)

I Thessalonians 4:5 – *And not for the mere gratification of his passions, like the Gentiles who know nothing of God.* (TCNT, also MNT & RSV)

II Timothy 2:22 – Flee from the passions of youth, but run after righteousness, faith, love, and peace, in company with those who out of a pure heart call upon the Lord. (MNT)

II Timothy 3:3 – *Without natural affection, implacable, slanderers, of unsubdued passions, savage, having no love for what is good.* (DBY)

II Timothy 3:6 – *For among them are to be found those who creep into homes and captivate weak women – women who, loaded with sins, and slaves to all kinds of passions.* (TCNT)

Titus 2:12 – *Training us to renounce irreligion and worldly passions, and to live sober, upright, and godly lives in this world.* (RSV, also MNT)

Titus 3:3 – *For we ourselves were once foolish, disobedient, led astray, slaves to various passions and pleasures, passing our days in malice and envy, hated by men and hating one another.* (RSV, also TCNT)

James 1:14 – *But when a man is tempted, it is his own passions that carry him away and serve as a bait.* (WNT, also TCNT)

James 1:15 – *Then Passion conceives and gives birth to Sin, and Sin, on reaching maturity, brings forth Death.* (TCNT)

James 4:1 – *Where do the conflicts and quarrels that go on among you come from? Do they not come from your passions which are always making war among your bodily members?* (MNT, also YLT)

James 4:2 – *You covet things and yet cannot get them; you commit murder; you have passionate desires and yet cannot gain your end; you begin to fight and make war. You have not, because you do not pray.* (WNT)

James 4:3 – *You ask and do not receive, because you ask wrongly, to spend it on your passions.* (RSV)

I Peter 1:14 – *Be like obedient children; do not let your lives be shaped by the passions which once swayed you in the days of your ignorance.* (TCNT, also MNT & RSV)

I Peter 2:11 – *I beseech you, beloved, as pilgrims and exiles, to abstain from passions of the flesh that war upon your souls.* (MNT, also RSV)

I Peter 4:2 – *That in future you may spend the rest of your earthly lives, governed not by human passions, but by the will of God.* (WNT, also RSV & TCNT)

I Peter 4:3 – *Let the time that is past suffice for doing what the Gentiles like to do, living in licentiousness, passions, drunkenness, revels, carousing, and lawless idolatry.* (RSV)

II Peter 1:4 – *For it was through this that he gave us what we prize as the greatest of his promises, that through them you might participate in the divine nature, now that you have fled from the corruption in the world, resulting from human passions.* (TCNT, also RSV)

II Peter 2:10 – *Especially those who, following the promptings of their lower nature, indulge their polluting passions and despise all control. Audacious and self-willed, they feel no awe of the Mighty, maligning them.* (TCNT, also RSV)

II Peter 2:18 – *For, uttering loud boasts of folly, they entice with licentious passions of the flesh men who have barely escaped from those who live in error.* (RSV, also TCNT)

II Peter 3:3 – *But, above all, remember that, in the last days, men will come who make a mock at everything – men governed only by their own passions.* (WNT also RSV)

Jude 1:16 – *These are grumblers, malcontents, following their own passions, loud-mouthed boasters, flattering people to gain advantage.* (RSV, also MNT & WNT)

Jude 1:18 – *How they used to say to you, "In the last times there will be scoffers who will be led only by their godless passions."* (MNT, also RSV)

Revelation 14:8 – *Another angel, a second, followed, saying, "Fallen, fallen is Babylon the great, she who made all nations drink the wine of her impure passion."* (RSV)

Revelation 18:3 – *For all nations have drunk the wine of her impure passion, and the kings of the earth have committed fornication with her, and the merchants of the earth have grown rich with the wealth of her wantonness."* (RSV)

Teach All Nations Mission

Teach All Nations Mission (TAN) is a global evangelical educational ministry birthed from the teaching ministries of Delron and Peggy Shirley. The name for Teach All Nations Mission was chosen to carefully indicate the exact heart of the Shirleys' mission. TAN's commitment is to establish a solid biblical foundation in national pastors and leaders so they can help enrich their own people. This vision is being accomplished by holding national leadership conferences and publishing and distributing Christian teaching materials in English and their local languages.

Someone accurately observed concerning the revival that is occurring in many parts of our world today that it is a mile wide but only an inch deep – the result of energetic evangelism by both missionaries and local Christians. Sadly, there is a marked shortage of teachers who are taking the next step in fulfilling our Lord's directive to teach them how to observe all that He has commanded. Therefore, Teach All Nations Mission has literally taken the words of Christ from Matthew 28:19, "Teach all nations," as its motto and mission statement.

TAN's commitment is to deepen that revival by training the pastors and leaders who then go back and strengthen their congregations. TAN pays for the travel and lodging of handpicked leaders because Delron and Peggy want to invest into their lives but know that these third-world saints could never afford to come at their own expense. TAN always provides the meals for all the guests during these conferences. The ministry also furnishes solid Christian literature in their local language or in English for those who understand the language.

Delron and Peggy realize that the challenge is much bigger than what they can accomplish in person; therefore, they have determined to expand the scope of their vision. One area of expansion includes a scholarship fund that will allow selected individuals to obtain a formal education in solid Christian colleges and Bible schools or through correspondence courses. The ministry has also assisted in building a Christian school in Zimbabwe and a Bible college in Nepal. Additionally, Teach All Nations assists the pastors and leaders they work with in times of need such as the tsunami in Sri Lanka, the earthquake in Nepal, and hurricanes in Belize and in the Turks and Caicos Islands. More recently, the ministry supported suffering Christians in twelve different nations who lost their source of income during the shutdowns during the COVID-19 pandemic.

Your gifts to and prayers for Teach All Nations will help the Shirleys continue their outreach to Christian leadership around the world.

Teach All Nations Mission
3210 Cathedral Spires
Colorado Springs, CO 80904
719-685-9999
www.teachallnationsmission.com
teachallnations@msn.com

Books by Delron & Peggy Shirley

Bingo, a Fresh Look at Grace
Christmas Thoughts
Cornerstones of Faith
Daily Bible Study Series (Five-Volume Set)
Daily Ditties from Delron's Desk
(Eight Volumes Available)
Doctor Livingstone, I Presume
Don't Leave Home Without It
Finally, My Brethren
Getting More UMPH out of Your Bible
Going Deeper in Jesus
The Great Commission – Doable
The IN Factors
In This Sign Conquer
Interface
Israel, Key to Human Destiny
The Last Enemy
Lessons Along the Way
Lessons from the Life of David
Living for the End Times
Maturing into the Full Stature of Jesus Christ
Maximum Impact
No Longer Bound
The Non-Conformer's Trilogy
Of Kings and Prophets
Passion for the Harvest
People Who Make A Difference
Positioned for Blessing and Power
Problem People of the Bible
Seeds and Harvest
The Seventh Man at the Well
So Send I You
So, You Wanna be a Preacher
Thirty-, Sixty-, One-Hundred-Fold
Tread Marks
Turning the World Upside Down and Back Again

Verse for the Day (Four Volumes Available)
Women for the Harvest
You'll be Darned to Heck
if You Don't Believe in Gosh
You Can Be Healed
Your Home Can Survive in the 21st Century
Your Part in the Grand Scheme of Things

Available at:
teachallnationsmission.com

www.ingramcontent.com/pod-product-compliance
Lightning Source LLC
LaVergne TN
LVHW051058080426
835508LV00019B/1942